BEYOND THE YELLOW BRICK ROAD

A STORY OF COURAGE

Barbara J. Mosher

AmErica House
Baltimore

First printing

All drawings by the author

ISBN: 1-58851-863-9
PUBLISHED BY AMERICA HOUSE BOOK PUBLISHERS
www.publishamerica.com
Baltimore

Printed in the United States of America

This book is dedicated to my husband Ron
who walked this road with me.

ACKNOWLEDGEMENTS

My heartfelt thanks to my husband Ron who laboriously typed, re-typed and computerized the entire manuscript.

I especially want to thank my brother-in-law Terry Mosher who gave his wisdom in editing the book, to Kris Butts my daughter who proofread and gave helpful hints, to my sisters Bette Croft and Peg Haley who helped with the chronology of events and to my sister-in-law Mary Mosher for her astute comments. Also many thanks to my son Todd Amy Trickett and Patti Chadwick for their technical help and encouragement.

You were my much needed support group.

Most of all, if there is anything in this book that ministers to you, it did not come from me but from the inspiration of the Holy Spirit. To God be the glory!

Scripture quotations are from the *Holy Bible*: the New International Version and the King James Version.

TABLE OF CONTENTS

INTRODUCTION

"----whose names are in the book of life"
(Philippians 4:3)

We read that the names of God's fellow workers are written in heaven in the *Book of Life.* That draws us to imagine a huge heavenly book, opened by an angel who reads down a long list of names to see if our name is on the list. But this book is more than simply a directory of names. It is not the "book of names," rather it is the book of LIFE. And each name there signifies a whole life; everything you have lived through – your birth, your joys and struggles, and ah, yes, your coming to God, to Jesus. Your name signifies all that you are, were, or ever will be. All there in the book of life, for God to read. Our story is God's story, with us, written in His book.

Were any of us to write our life story it would take volumes to tell it all. And it would be intertwined with the stories of all those whose lives are interwoven with ours. For this reason I am choosing one story of mine to tell, the story of my daughter Charmaine and myself. I picked out our story together because mothers have a closeness with their children's lives that is very special, perhaps because we spend so much time with them when they're little. It results in a soul bonding of some sort. We certainly see this in the life of Jesus with his mother, whose presence weaves a thread of bonding throughout his whole life.

Certainly, I always felt that there was some sort of soul thing between Charmaine and myself. I think that was because of the affinity I felt with her in her sufferings, and from that depth, conversely the joy I felt with her in her joys.

7

As I look back I can see how God used and directed our life experiences, back and forth with each other, in the weaving of our "names" into His book.

So I begin.

Chapter 1

Saying Good-bye

"Precious in the sight of the Lord is the death of his saints"
(Psalm 116:15)

That February day was crisp and cold with a light snow falling.

As we drove into the cemetery we spotted the canopy under which we would soon all gather to say our last good-bye to our beloved daughter and sister, Charmaine.

Stepping out of the car, the coldness struck my face and I couldn't help but remember that this was the sort of day that Char liked best; a day to get the horses out and take them for a run.

I wondered about Ron, my husband of thirty-three years, as we walked arm in arm to stand before the casket. Neither of us spoke. We had each been caught up in our own private grief, each with our own personal memories.

Later Ron related:

It seemed like I was just watching things happen, almost as if it wasn't real. This was not supposed to be happening. Maybe in the movies but not in real life. At least not to me. Emotionally I caved in, from all the tragic experiences we had gone through. This should have been the closure, the time to say good-bye, that everything is done, that she is put to rest, and her spirit is in heaven with our Lord. But for me, this was not getting done.

I was troubled about the mix-up in the grave sites, and that Char was not, on that day, taken care of properly.

****

My attention was pulled to the elderly pastor who was beginning the committal service. His large black fur hat and long black coat made him look like a Russian Cossack. He was reading a poem about our loved one not being gone, but just in another room. Perhaps. But a room we could not enter.

Not in this life.

Our seven other children stood in sentinel around their sister's casket.

Kris, our oldest daughter, was caught up in her own struggle with recently diagnosed multiple sclerosis. Was her grief focused on her sister's life being cut so short?

Kris:

I didn't remember an awful lot about Char's life because I was so much involved in my own life. I thought that she was very strong and handled everything very well. I knew she'd go to heaven because she was a Christian.

****

Kris' husband Gary stood sadly beside, shaking his head. He had loved Char too, in a perfect love that aroused neither jealousy nor thoughts of infidelity, only of compassion for a close friend.

Mark was next, our oldest son, who lived farthest away. His urgent phone calls always inquired, "Do you think I should come down again to see her, Mom?"

Now he was caught in his own private grief.

Mark:

One profound revelation came to me with the death of my sister Charmaine. As much as it was a terrible loss, I was nevertheless relieved that her suffering was over. Over the last two years of her life she had remained valiantly optimistic even as her body continued to fail, but it had been a long, steady, downhill progression. This wasn't a sudden, unexpected parting. We had seen her struggle and fight a long and, toward the end, inevitably losing battle for a long time. The impotence of watching someone you love move towards death was difficult to face. As much as it affected everyone in the family, I know it took a heavy toll on mom and dad.

I remember seeing my father hunched wearily in front of a large window in a hospital lounge framed there as if he were a permanent fixture. I think it was the day Charmaine had died and everyone was traveling to meet my parents there. As the two of us spoke alone, he took a deep sigh and said, "This has been the worst year of my life." I'm sure it was.

****

Cal was there. I remembered his closeness to Char. A photograph of them crossed my mind; a little brother and sister in a field of dandelions, both holding big bouquets, his arm around her, big grins on their faces.

During Char's last hospital stay Cal had bought her a solid gold chain necklace, wanting to show in his own way the love he held for her.

Cal:

Her death and the way I felt is just too personal to talk about.

In the family line-up, Char's younger brother Todd stood by with tears. His wife Sarah had been to the funeral with him but was unable to come to the committal service as she had to take care of their infant son.

****

Seeing him standing there I recalled that awful day, (was it only 3 days ago?) that Ron and I hunted him up in his college classroom, calling him out in the hall to give him the bad news that his sister was gone.

What was he thinking?

Todd:

I was reminiscing about our childhood; thinking about some of the mean pranks I'd played on Char and about how I'd teased her. Now I felt bad. I remembered the time in the hayloft of the barn when we'd covered a hole lightly with hay. When she came running after us she fell in and the hay bales fell in on top of her. A big joke. She could've got hurt. Now Char was gone. I felt a sadness.

****

Gloria, blond and slim, was putting a flower on the casket. She had been Char's close comrade all those years in their adventures at the barn with the horses and their menagerie of small animals.

Away at college, her cheery and humorous letters and home-made cards had kept Char smiling.

Gloria:
The thing I remember most about Char is how encouraging she was. She was always telling me "You can do it!" When I went out for the hurdles in track, even thought Cal helped me, Char was my main influence. I always thought I would live close to her. Now she was gone. I felt loss and sadness.

Red-haired Russ ached my heart most of all. Tall, gangly, sixteen, he had spent time every day talking with Char in her room after she had been forced to come home from college to live.

Russ hadn't cried in front of us until he saw his older brothers cry. I hoped that somebody would come forth to help him get through this. Russ had gone into a shell and there was nothing we could do to reach him.

Yesterday he had sat in Char's empty room rocking silently in her rocking chair.

****

Russ answers:
I was shocked. I had no idea that Char was going to die. I couldn't believe it. She had been very sick before and had pulled out of it Ok. Why hadn't anyone told me that she was going to die? I would have liked to have gone up to the hospital to be with her more often. Now she was gone.

****

Lastly was Andrea, twelve years old, who had cried out to me one day in anguish after watching Char's suffering, "I wish she would die. It would be better for her just to die."

Andrea said:
I remember how strong and brave she was. She had such a calm spirit and seemed touched by God. She had a great sense of humor and was always giggling with me. When the principal came in my

classroom, I knew she had died. I was glad that she was released and wasn't suffering anymore. I still feel her very close to me.

****

Now the service was over.
We all hugged each other.
As Ron and I left arm in arm, I wondered if he was still angry at God. It was too painful for him to talk about Char.

Chapter 2

Just Like Robin

"Do not worry about tomorrow"
Jesus (Matt. 6:34)

Charmaine Carol was born the day after Christmas, December 26, 1960, our Christmas baby, our fifth child. We brought her home to her sister Kris, aged 6, and brothers Mark 3 ½, and Cal 1 ½..

We had lost our second child, a little girl named Robin, almost four years earlier, after what seemed like an insignificant accident. It had happened on a Christmas holiday. She had tumbled off our bed, bumping her head. That night she slipped into a coma. Despite brain surgery the next day, the doctors were unable to save her. The surgeon had found massive bleeding that he could not stop. Specialists told us, in lay terms, that she was a bleeder, unusual in a female.

We had persevered in prayer and in faith that she would live. When she died I felt that God had not answered my prayers and was far away. Grief filled me for a long time.

In concern over the possibility of other children being bleeders, our sons Mark and Cal, as infants, prior to circumcision, had had their blood tested to check on the possibility of bleeding disorders. The test results showed in each one a normal clotting time.

Now we had a new baby girl! Our spirits soared.

Char's outstanding feature was her large blue eyes. My sister remarked on it and took picture after picture of this baby with the bright blue eyes.

But before she was a month old Ron and I began to be very

15

frightened. As our beloved baby laid in her bassinet swinging her arms, her hands would hit the sides, causing large black and blue spots.

Bruises. Just like Robin. Robin had bruised easily. We were plunged into fear. How would Char ever live? Would the first mishap take her life?

I knew from experience with three other lively children that we couldn't watch her every minute.

So I mourned.

If I mourned, my little Charmaine was oblivious to it. She laughed and cooed despite my teardrops falling on her face. A happy baby. The thought came to me that I could waste my whole life in mourning. Maybe she would grow up and be strong and well and happy. And I would have wasted my whole life in mourning.

Jesus' words came. "Therefore, do not worry about tomorrow, for tomorrow will worry about itself. Each day has enough trouble of its own" (Matt. 6:34). In other words, live one day at a time.

I looked at Char in her little basket, sleeping. Today she would be alright. Nothing would happen to her today.

So I survived one day at a time. One step at a time. Follow the yellow brick road. One step at a time. Like Dorothy going to Oz.

When Charmaine was a year old she weighed enough for the doctors at the Buffalo Children's Hospital to take a large enough volume of her blood to complete their testing of her.

Then came the diagnosis.

"She has severe vonWillebrand's disease," the blood specialist said, "It's a type of hemophilia, very much like classic hemophilia, and affects girls as well as boys. There is no treatment for it except blood transfusions for trauma.

Oh yes, her blood type is rare, B neg. There is only one person listed in your county with that type of blood. Keep an eye on her. Protect her against falls. But let her live a normal life.

Only one in three people with this disease are able to cope well with life. One-third of the people withdraw from active life. About one third go the other way and challenge life with risky and dangerous behavior. About one third live well."

Ron and I looked at Charmaine's bright blue eyes and knew that she was going to do well. She had survived the first year of life. Already she was a very determined individual. Those bright eyes told us she was going to make it.

As we left the hospital a woman came in carrying a listless child whose coloring was a deep gray-blue. We passed another child whose head hung to the side and whose eyes showed no ability to learn. Still a third was missing a leg.

Despite the blow we had received, we walked out the door with our baby, feeling blessed.

Chapter 3

The Ax Overhead

"What I feared has come upon me"
(Job 3:25)

Despite feeling blessed, my old enemy, FEAR, dogged my steps. I knew that the first hard bump Charmaine had might be the end of her. God had let it happen once. It could happen again. I was unsure of God. And so I lived with "the ax hanging over my head," waiting for it to fall on us.

The day came when Char took that hard bump. She was 15 months old. I was downstairs cooking oatmeal for the children for breakfast. (funny that I remember it was oatmeal). Suddenly we heard a crash over-head; upstairs in Char's room. She had somehow wadded up her blankets and climbed up over the top of her crib bars, crashing to the floor.

We rushed her to the hospital emergency room, expecting the worst. Surprisingly, there was not a mark on her, or a symptom of distress. Our pediatrician, under our urging, kept her overnight in the hospital for observation. I remember his kind comment at our wonder over her having no signs of trauma.

"Perhaps the good Lord put his hand out and caught her," he said.

Yes, indeed it was strange. There was no mark on her.

When we brought her home I sat upstairs on our bed thinking. Puzzling. Realizing, that the life and death of this child was not in my hands. See. She took a bad fall. See, she is OK. I had thought her life was in my hands. It was not. It was in God's hands.

I was filled with relief. Maybe she would survive. I loved her so. Maybe things would be alright.

I had just found out I was pregnant again. It was a surprise. I had been agonizing over this pregnancy, wondering, "How can I ever take care of Charmaine and a new baby?"

Now I knew that I would manage.

In looking back, I am glad that at that time when Todd was unborn there was no amniocentesis (insertion of a hollow needle through the abdominal wall and uterus of a pregnant woman to obtain amniotic fluid for chromosomal abnormalities) and no legal abortion available. My view of doctors was that they were all-wise and all-knowing; men to be highly respected and listened to.

I shudder to think that their so-called "superior" knowledge might have been used to influence us as candidates for abortion. If that had been so, we would have missed out on Todd, our wonderful son.

Todd was born January 14, 1963. He also was a bleeder.

We had always wanted a large family. Life was hectic, but full of joy and laughter. Ron was well on his way in his career as a teacher and high school football, basketball and track coach. Five children at home kept me busy.

From time to time there were difficulties with Charmaine and Toddy from tiny mouth cuts or from cutting teeth. They would start bleeding and it wouldn't stop. We tried ice. We tried popsicles. We tried calling the doctor. We tried topical preparations from the drugstore.

We watched a constant slow trickle of blood make a healthy child turn gray-pale and make her or him finally become listless, and sick to the stomach from swallowing blood.

After about 8 hours of bleeding we were afraid of the child going into shock. But just short of that, the bleeding would stop.

Instead of Char's bright blue eyes I would see her large eyes of suffering, looking at me to help, and there was so very little I could do.

Through experimentation Ron and I discovered that we could actually apply pressure to mouth cuts, holding on with our fingers to the child's tongue or lip. It was no easy task to restrain a wiggley 18 month old child. We had to wait until the child was feeling sick and weak.

Then Char or Todd would sit on our laps quietly while we rocked, sang, read stories or watched TV, while applying gentle pressure to the cut, with fingers that soon began to ache from immobility.

Kris:
I always felt sorry for Mom and Dad having to go through those hours of holding Char or Todd and trying to stop the bleeding. I remember thinking, "What a pain!"

****

Ron and I would spell each other, taking turns getting supper, looking after the other children and doing what had to be done. Sometimes we had to apply the mouth pressure on through the night. Often the bleeding would stop in the night, only to start up the next morning when the child attempted to eat some breakfast. Those were difficult times, but continuously applying pressure to a tongue or lip did keep the child from getting to that frightening stage of near shock.

Despite difficulties and fears, Ron and I decided to let Char and Todd grow up as normally as possible. We soon found out that being overly protective didn't help. They might avoid bumping the corner of the table, but trip over their own feet. Bumps from ordinary activities weren't predictable or preventable.

It was important to us not to crush the child's spirit. We wanted Char and Todd to be normal and so we took the risk and held our breath.

However, we were extra careful about some things.

The baby gate at the stairway was *never* left open. (The older kids soon learned how to swing over this narrow space). The extension bars on the baby crib were *always* put up.

The other children didn't seem to be too affected by the fact that Char and Todd had hemophilia and had to have special treatment. I remember one day, after Char at age three had just recovered from a bad mouth bleed, her big brother Mark, who was seven, came to talk to me about her. He seriously stated that Charmaine had an awful problem.

I thought, "Oh, oh, here it comes."

"Yes," he said belligerently, "Every time she sits next to me at the table, she kicks me."

So much for the big problem.

Gloria was born when Todd was 2 ½ years. (If you have lost track, she was our seventh child). Gloria was not a bleeder.

At around age two she began to realize that she was not getting the full treatment for her hurts, which I just kissed away.

Char and Todd got cold cloths and ice packs for their bruises.

We all laughed when after a head bump Gloria came out of the bathroom with a soaking wet wash cloth on her head, the water running down her face, and a look that said, "If you won't give me the right treatment, I'll get it myself."

When she was about seven, Gloria lamented to me that she never had anything wrong with her. I had to take her in my arms and tell her that I was so happy that I had a strong and healthy little girl and that it was wonderful.

For the most part, the children took the difficulties of Char and Todd as a normal course of events. It was just a way of life.

Cal:
Char's disabilities never seemed to hamper her. She always seemed able to do the things she wanted to do.

****

Gloria:
I always thought that Char's hemophilia experiences were kind of neat, because it was different. When she got older, the home transfusions were cool.

Chapter 4

Pain and More Pain

"In this world you will have trouble"
(John 16:33)

Char was always a very determined little girl. She was strong willed and very active - a go-getter.

When she was about five years old she began to have trouble with bleeding into her left ankle joint. We didn't know why. Perhaps just a slightly twisted ankle started it off. This was extremely painful because the bleeding and swelling would not stop until that small space was so packed with blood that it created its own pressure and shut it off.

This was so painful that she screamed and cried and moaned. It was too painful to apply ice-packs, so we would suspend her foot and ankle in ice water. She would go to sleep that way at night with her leg hanging off the bed.

I remember her lying there turning her head back and forth, saying in a monotone voice, "My ankle hurts. My ankle hurts."

She couldn't have aspirin and the doctor was afraid to order narcotics for fear of eventual addiction.

I would try to comfort her, to no avail. Lying in my bed at night, listening to her, I was filled with emotional pain and fear, and prayed desperately.

Our pediatrician didn't really know how to treat the hemophilia, so he often avoided treating it. Several times he did order a blood product; fresh frozen plasma, sent down from Buffalo, but by the time it was administered, it didn't seem to do any good.

At that time we got connected up with the Hemophilia Center in Rochester, NY. The orthopedic doctor grinned when Char, in her bright red jumper, walked across the room, twirling around. "How'd you ever get in this fraternity?" he quipped, noting that the classic hemophilia patients were all males.

Over time his grin faded when he tried one thing after another, attempting to stop the chronic, damaging bleeding into her ankle. First crutches, then an ankle brace made of metal, with leather straps up to the knee, to hold the ankle immobile and prevent deformity.

I remember the day that Charmaine was fitted to the brace. After it was put on her and we started home, she sat in the back seat of the car whining and crying. The straps pinched. Already bruises were starting. She hated it. She wasn't going to wear it. She cried and cried. We drove that long way home with heavy hearts.

We arrived home just as the school bus was pulling up in front of our house and her brothers, sisters and all the neighbor kids were getting off. Char went out on the front porch and called cheerily, "Hey, everybody, come and see my new brace!" She had the whole neighborhood interested. One little friend even wanted to try it on.

Wearing the brace to school was another matter. Little girls wore dresses to school then, and so the bulky metal brace was very obvious. Char came home disturbed. All the kids at school had gathered around her in a circle, staring at her and the brace. I gently told her that they were just interested or curious. They had never seen a brace before. Day after day this was a trial for Char, until one day, in desperation I blurted out, "Oh, they just don't know any better!" That ended it. The fault was theirs, not hers.

Despite the brace, the ankle continued to bleed. She had to continually use crutches, which caused bruising under her arms, so she often resorted to crawling. One day I came home with groceries to find Char and the neighbor kids crawling around the grass. "What are you doing?" I asked. "Playing lion" came back the answer with smiles.

In a big family there was always work to be done. One of Char's jobs was to crawl around pushing a cardboard box, picking up toys. She did her share.

A year went by. The ankle got no better. Every treatment failed. I prayed and prayed for her ankle to heal. The x-ray looked worse, "like the arthritic joint of a 75 year old," the doctor said. I began to despair, "She'll never walk again." This lively, spirited child was never going to walk again.

"You of little faith --- Why are you so afraid?" (Jesus: Matt.8:26). But I had believed once, and something had gone wrong. Gloom settled over me.

God sends people. Usually not in the way we would pick. Judie had kids the age of some of ours. She looked at Char and her bruises with a grin and said, "Who bashed you in the ribs?"

I thought, "How callous. Surely she sees how bad this is. Doesn't she care?" The jibes continued. "Who clunked you on the forehead? Is that a bruise or just dirt?" We began to laugh. We laughed and laughed. We joined in. "Is that spaghetti on your face, or is your mouth bleeding? I see you cut your finger. Don't bleed all over the living-room rug. Get out in the kitchen!"

It lost its power over us. The monster was cut down by humor. We took the attitude, "If this is funny I don't care who sees it, or says anything about it." We nicknamed Todd "the petekei kid" as he was covered from neck to knees with these little pinpoint purple spots from crawling in and out of cardboard boxes at play.

We started going to church regularly. No sooner did I sit in the pew than the organ would play the first hymn and tears would run down my face.

There was still a rift between me and God over Robin's death. My heart cried out, "Why? Why did you let Robin die when you could have saved her?" I wanted to run up to the altar and throw myself on my knees and cry out, "Jesus carried a cross, and Jesus suffered, but he knew why. But why God, for Robin? What good did it do?"

The people in the choir would look at me and see me crying. Every Sunday. I felt so embarrassed and humiliated. I wanted to hide.

I didn't receive any comfort or sympathy from the people in church. If they felt it, they didn't show it. Nobody put an arm around me or prayed with me. Not even the minister.

The congregation seemed very formal and uncomfortable around me.

A rumor came back to me that it was said that I was a "super-sensitive" person. The best that happened was that one woman would look me sadly in the eyes and say that she'd be thinking of me.

I needed so much spiritual help to get through this ordeal. I felt that the church should have been the place to offer it, but at that time they didn't.

Chapter 5

Looking Up

"He restoreth my soul"
(Psalm 23:3)

When Charmaine was nine years old, two important things happened. One, she had a Sunday School teacher who brought her to the Lord. She entered into a real relationship with God. Two, she fell in love with animals.

On the first count, when God became real to her, she received great strength to endure. And not only to endure but to go beyond endurance. Most children bounce back after an injury, but Char actually seemed to gain from it. She had much less fear over her struggles than I did. I saw that she had something in her life that I didn't have, God in her life in a very real way. I had to look at it. She began to have a depth of soul that most children don't have. She was very brave. She would cry about having sore arms from the crutches, but when the bus came, off to school she would go on them.

Secondly, when she was nine years old she got a kitten. Ron hates cats. He was adamant, "I will not have a cat in this house." But somehow, one got in. Little girls have a way with their Dads. That was just the beginning of a menagerie of animals that we were to have over the years. In time it included white mice, hamsters, gerbils, rabbits, dogs, horses and even a ferret.

I have a memory of Charmaine sitting with her nose pressed into the wire of her rabbit's cage. The rabbit would come up and press his wet little nose against hers. They were "communicating" she said.

Our family ran much like other large families; picnics, vacations, school achievements, concerts, ball games and more ball games, visits to relatives, supper around the kitchen table, bedtime stories, favorite TV shows, slumber parties, birthday celebrations, home-made Halloween costumes, daily work, and interspersed in it all, trips to the hospitals and clinics. We practiced routine home medical care which we developed from experience. What appeared as extremely difficult to observers, was just a part of life to us.

Char wore the brace for about three years. It didn't seem to help. The orthopedic doctor became angry and suspicious that I wasn't following his instructions. But I was following them to the letter of the law.

I began to see that doctors were not God. When the orthopedic doctor wanted to try an experimental process, I said no. The brace had already failed to stop the chronic bleeding into her ankle, and I wasn't convinced that more extensive bracing would help.

I was the front-runner in making many of these decisions because I was the one who spent a great deal of time with the children at home and the one who took them to clinics and hospitals. However, Ron and I became an expert medical team in handling crisis, each with our own area of duty. I made the phone calls. He got the car ready and carried the child out. Most of all we gave each other moral support and understanding during these tough times.

Char's ankle was healed in a strange way. She got hepatitis B, no doubt from some transfusions she had taken. She was very sick and had to be hospitalized for a while and then came home and laid on the couch for six weeks. Our very lively, wiggly little girl was, for once, very quiet. It gave her ankle the rest it needed. When she gradually got better we first limited her to walking only across the room and back. Then, we very slowly increased the walks, and joy of joys, the ankle held up! We held our breath.

When we returned to the orthopedic clinic at the Hemophilia center, the doctor was delighted with Char's progress. A bevy of medical students stood around the examining table as the doctor expounded on the use of the brace as the deciding factor. I wanted to shout out, "No, no, it wasn't the brace. God healed her ankle," but I didn't dare speak up.

Charmaine never had any serious trouble with that ankle again. God had answered my prayer. "Oh you of little faith. Why did you fear?"

Chapter 6

A Curse Or A Blessing?

**"Consider it pure joy, my brothers,whenever you face trials of
many kinds"
(James 1:2)**

When our oldest son Mark was twelve years old he became
diabetic. That was another ordeal to live with and struggle through.

Our youngest son, red-haired, Russell, was born Nov. 24, 1969,
at the same time Mark was in the hospital getting regulated to
insulin. Taking care of a brand new baby and adjusting to the rigors
of managing Mark's diabetes, took every ounce of our emotional and
physical energy. Nevertheless, as we had done with the hemophilia,
we struggled to fit this disease into our normal life-style. We always
tried to minimize the disease, relegating it to a place of "necessary
annoyance" but not "super-importance" in the child's life.

Mark did very well and excelled at sports in his school career.
However, it was not easy, and what was equally hard was that three
years later when Charmaine turned twelve, she became diabetic also.

I felt that God was cursing my family---cursing my children.
Charmaine had gone through so much pain and suffering and now to
have diabetes. It seemed like too much. I lamented this to my mother.
She replied, "No, God doesn't curse people. He is not cursing you.
He has given you these children because he knows that you can care
for them.." I was strengthened and went to the hospital to see Char.

She must have sensed the heavy burden on me, for when I entered the room she was glad to see me, and enthusiastic, yes, enthusiastic, about giving her own insulin shots. "I'm gonna give my own shots, Mom." She had all the nurses amazed at her. Even the bruises caused by each insulin injection didn't dampen her spirits. I may have been dragging, but she came home on top of it all.

On May 18, 1973, our last child, Andrea Elizabeth, was born, a beautiful, dark haired baby girl. A blood test showed her to be a bleeder also. By now I was more confident that children with hemophilia could grow up and weather the problems associated with it. New and better treatment was out, and our doctors and nurses were getting educated in how to administer it.

Fortunately, our children were good in school. They won awards and got into all kinds of activities. Char learned to play the clarinet and piano and played the organ at church. As she grew older she went to competition for the clarinet and was in All-County Chorus and All-County band.

Char's love of animals continued. Her sentiments were expressed in this prayer that she wrote in her sixth grade Sunday School Class:

O Lord, please forgive me and everyone else in the world, for all our sins. Help us to do the right things, and for us to have great faith in you and know that you are with us all the time and are taking care of us. Show us God, how to take care of your animals and make them comfortable and love them no matter in what conditions we or they are in. Thank you, O God, for the glory you put in the world for us to enjoy. Thank you for everything you've done for me and everyone else in the world.

In Jesus' name we pray.

Amen

Chapter 7

The Horse

"Delight yourself in the Lord
and he will give you the desires of your heart"
(Psalm 37:4)

Charmaine's love of animals continued. Our next door neighbors had horses for their children. They maintained a large barn down the road with perhaps six Morgan horses. But their children had grown up and left home or lost interest in the horses.

Char, however, began to spend all her free time down at the barn, working with the hired man, grooming the horses and dreaming dreams about actually owning *a horse* some day.

Char wrote in her journal:

Oct. 22, 1973 Monday
I really want a horse, but I don't know if I could really take care of one. I'll have to see if God thinks it's best. I hope so!

Oct. 23, 1973 Tuesday
God, if I don't give up my life for you, I wouldn't be able to face heaven. God, I want a horse, I really do. I have beautiful visions of riding a free horse, just jumping on it and taking off, but if my thought is from the devil, I wouldn't get a horse for anything.

Nov. 1, 1973 Thursday
Today my friend Jeanne and I went down to the barn. We brush the five mares every time, they're all sleek and shiny. Jeanne wants to get a horse too I asked Mrs. Taylor how much it would cost to keep a horse at their barns. She said, 2 dollars a day for stalls and 1 dollar a day for pasture. My heart sank. But it then soared because she said if me and Jeanne could get a horse that we could keep them there free, if we worked there. We told our parents and prayed.

Char and her friends were given the use of a little room upstairs in the barn. There they kept their treasures, yes, animals; pigeons, white mice, gerbils, and rabbits. Of course a cat and dog added to the barn family.

Shy and gentle sister Gloria became a part of the group involved in the animal adventures at the barn. Their lives seemed to be wrapped up in the cycle of events in the life and death of these little creatures that they kept.

One summer day I climbed up the ladder to that little loft room. There on the rickety table beside the animal cages I saw a piece of paper. I picked it up to read, "God is always here." Guarding their treasures, no doubt. If only I had learned that earlier, "God is always here."

Char got great comfort from the barn. It was her refuge. From time to time she had painful joint bleeds and had to go to the hospital for transfusions. It was always an ordeal. She would come home on crutches, weak and tired. I would want her to lie down and rest, but no, she insisted on immediately going down to the barn. She'd limp or trudge or even use her crutches to go down the back road to the barn, and there she would stay the rest of the day with her animals. There she would work, feeding the horses, doing what she could.

When she came home she'd be restored. Her body would still be in bad shape but her spirits would be up.

About this time Ron and I did something, in the eyes of many people, that was an extremely foolish thing. We bought Charmaine a horse for her combined Christmas/ thirteenth birthday gift. Don't ask me what we were thinking of. There was an ad in the paper for a horse for sale, $100.00. We got it.

Char wrote in her journal:

Christmas Eve 1973
I cried half the night, I knew we couldn't afford a horse and it was impossible anyway.
Christmas
I got a suitcase, 6 glass cats, a sketching book, pen and ink from Kris, posters from Jeanne. I thought, well Merry Christmas stupid, make the best of it. I was downhearted.

Then my father gave me this letter:

Dear Char,
I'm sorry that I can't be with you around the Christmas tree this morning. My name is Cindy and I have a brown coat almost the same color as yours.
For the past couple of years I have been quite lonely with no one to come and play with me. They tell me you like animals and I sure like little girls.
When you get a minute or two why don't you grab an apple or two and come down to the barn to see me, I'm quite anxious to meet you. I live in the last stall on the right, you can't miss me.
Your friend and horse
Cindy
Merry Christmas Char, and a Happy Birthday.

Later Char wrote:

I couldn't believe it. I ran upstairs and got dressed. I cut a big apple and ran down to the barn. I don't know what I expected, but my heart jumped when I saw her. She was a great big 13 year old American Saddle Horse. I loved her.

When this huge animal was delivered to the barn the evening before Christmas, Ron and I looked at the horse in fear, and then at each other, and said, "What have we done?"

If we had fears, Char didn't. "Cindy" was the joy of her life. The best present ever to be had. It was a Christmas morning we will never forget. Everyone trudged down to the barn to see the spectacle. The "ohs." The "ahs." This was the answered prayer. Char and her friend Jeanne had been talking "horse" and fervently praying for one for years.

We had talked to our neighbors; the doctor and his wife, and now Char arranged that if she took care of their six horses, then she'd get her horse's room and board free.

We simply didn't have enough money to support a horse.

Cindy was like a part of the family. We all took an interest. We all learned to ride. It was a happy time.

For the doctors at the Hemophilia Center it was not a happy time but one of adamant disagreement with us. A horse was too dangerous. It was foolish. They had given us many logical reasons against it. But we went heart over head and got it anyway. Finally a compromise was made. Char would wear a football helmet when she rode. She didn't mind wearing it. She had the horse!

Horses have expenses, unexpected by green horns like us. Cindy needed shoes. We could hardly keep up with shoes for our eight children much less a horse.

Charmaine found out that the school was starting oratorical contests. And those contests offered prize money to the winner, first prize $100.00. Char signed up and worked on her speech. She overcame her nervousness of speaking in public, got up in the high-school auditorium, and speaking on religion and values, won the first prize. She proudly came home with the money and Cindy got her shoes.

Oh, if life could only stay on the top-side. But mother nature took her turn and Char became a young lady. Not without troubles. The beginning of menses meant hemorrhaging and hospital stays. Sometimes transfusions helped and sometimes they didn't. The result was weakness, severe anemia and the need for iron injections. Every month was an ordeal, and sometimes one month ran into the next without relief. Consequently we spent a lot of time in hospital emergency rooms, either at the Olean General, 15 miles away, or for more serious things, the Rochester General 100 miles away. Birth control pills were finally prescribed which helped the problem somewhat, but they tended to make her feel nauseous.

We found that very few medical people knew how to treat the

problems, and so they relied upon us for help. We were quickly able to discern what was effective and what wasn't.

Todd was not without his difficulties with the hemophilia. Wanting to take part in athletics as his older brothers did and be admired by his father/coach, he tried several sports, only to be overcome by serious joint bleeds.

During this time Ron and I took turns managing the family and running Char and Todd to the Rochester hospital. Often the older children watched the younger ones while we took off in the flurry of a snowstorm heading for Rochester with a pain-wracked child in the back seat. Sometimes in spelling each other, one of us would return home exhausted with the treated child, only to find our anxious spouse at the door, waiting to take the next hurting child for treatment.

Despite the hard times there were often three or four months at a time of trouble-free living.

Since we had a large family, and the household was set up around children, it was a real pleasure for us to invite other children to join it. Over the years we had three different children stay with us in the summertime through the Fresh-Air program. We also hosted three Exchange students in different years; two from Brazil and one from Belgium.

When Marcelo, a high school student from Brazil, spent his first night with us, we woke him up in the night to tell him that we were taking Todd to the hospital in Rochester and probably wouldn't be home until the next day, but the other kids would help him get off to school.

Marcelo was ever amazed that we took our crises so calmly. He would often remark, in his Brazilian accent, "How can you do that?"

Chapter 8

The Healings

"I am the Lord who heals you"
(Exodus 15:26)

Ron and I were an expert medical team but we hadn't put the time into our marriage relationship that we should have. Heavy marriage problems began to weigh on us. We were drawing far apart; he with his heavy schedule of work and coaching, and me with the children, and their medical problems, and my growing spirit of discontent over everything. No longer did my life bring me fulfillment. Something important was missing. The old intimate things that had been good between us no longer were. We were strangers each in a different world. I blamed Ron, thinking that he wasn't interested or understanding of me. And then I blamed myself, thinking I just did not have the love or feelings for Ron that I felt I should have. I felt pitifully inadequate, and even angry at him that he no longer inspired those loving emotions in me.

I tried analyzing our marriage to figure out what was wrong. I tried to make changes in our communication process. When Ron didn't respond the way I wanted him to, I became discouraged and angry.

Nothing I tried seemed to help.

I went through the motions in our marriage, but my heart cried out for something more.

I started taking college courses, one a semester, to add something new to my life.

Kris and Mark had graduated and left home , making me realize that some day all the children would be gone, and I would want something to do. Still, despite my interest in college, something was missing. Guilt set in, for I knew I had many blessings in life and should be happy.

In agony over the mess of our marriage, I knelt alone in our room one morning and committed my life entirely into God's hands.

I shuddered with fear because I imagined that something terrible would happen to us, or to our children, that would bring us back together. But in my despair over our relationship I made that commitment to God anyway.

We were going to church and the new, young pastor was preaching messages that touched my heart. I was doing a lot of thinking about God.

Then one night I woke up in the middle of the night feeling strange; like I was coming apart in the middle. Something was happening. It crossed my mind that I might be dying, but strangely that thought did not disturb me.

Then the great light of God seemed to be in the room, and in my soul. Waves of love and joy beyond description poured over me. God was real! In the light of dawn that day I wanted to run outdoors and down the street shouting to everyone, "Hey! God is real! He's really here. And He loves you. He loves me."

Many things happened at that time. The teachings of Jesus that I had learned in church and Sunday school jumped into focus. Suddenly I knew with assurance what Jesus meant, what he was teaching, and how it applied to life. I was filled with joy. This must be the Holy Spirit. This must be what other people talked about. Oh yes! I knew it – at last!

The rift between myself and God over Robin's death was healed by God. I had never understood why God had let Robin die. For years I had cried out, "Why?," but God did not answer.

Then I had rationalized, that she might have been badly impaired had she lived, or that I wouldn't have been able to endure it, or that we might not have had the other children if she had been an ever constant care.

Even though these were logical answers they did not answer my heart's cry to God. My pain and disappointment had remained, even though I had pushed it to the back of my mind.

Eighteen years later, in this time of being held in an awareness of the perfect love of God, Robin's death came back to the foreground.

The next night I experienced the events of her death over again, only this time God took me through it in his love.

I re-lived her fall, the trip to the hospital, the doctors, the nurses, everything, even holding her still little body in my arms after she died.

With each new picture my tears flowed, but not in agony. Something was happening. A healing was taking place. I didn't have to know "why" anymore. God's love was enough. Somehow that which had been my agony with the Lord was also what brought me close to the Lord.

God simply forgave me for never being able to forgive him. Then I could forgive myself. My joy was complete.

Ron saw me bubbling over with joy and laughter. He looked at me with strange eyes. I tried to explain to him what had happened to me. He felt threatened. He was glad for me, but what did it have to do with him? It drove a further wedge between us.

I was so gloriously in the clouds that nothing could daunt me. I wrote and wrote and felt an eagerness to read the Bible and to join a Bible study group at church.

Ron and I went to our pastor concerning our marriage problems. He counseled us to go to a minister in Rochester who specialized in marriage counseling, and so we did. For the best part of a year, this man, wonderfully used of God, struggled with us to get our marriage back together. We came to the conclusion that we could live with our differences. The pressure was off.

Then, some time later we went on a marriage encounter weekend and that "put the frosting back on the cake." Ron received a special blessing from the Lord on that weekend, and he was no longer threatened by my involvement with religion, but became an active part of it.

Char wrote in her journal:

My parents had a good time at their retreat. I could tell just by the way they talked and looked. They're really happy. I'm really glad.

I began to see through God's perspective. The hemophilia our children had did not loom as such a big thing anymore. It was as if God took me way up high in the sky and let me look down and see through his eyes. From that viewpoint I saw our children that had the hemophilia. The hemophilia was there, but it was really very small. Compared to God's power it was minute. The great burden of their hemophilia was lifted off my shoulders. God was in charge. The ax of fear, that always hung over our heads, was gone.

A sense of humor came to me. Everything seemed so funny. As I had wept tears of relief during the emotional healing of Robin's death, I now laughed and laughed.

Nature took on a new dimension of beauty. I found the unfolding of spring to be breathtaking. Joy of joys, the emptiness was filled.

Charmaine noticed the difference in me. She made me a booklet of beautiful pictures cut out of magazines and captions under them. One of them was, "You find joy in everyday things!" I began to be able to talk to her about God.

About that time Char was struggling with constant wrist joint bleeds. It had begun when she got a clarinet and practiced a great deal on it, every afternoon sitting on the back steps after school. She was going to master that instrument or else! She did become proficient at it, but at cost to her wrist. The bleeds were so often and required immobilization that she learned to write with her right hand. (She was a lefty).

Char had a recurring dream that she called "The tortures." In this dream she was going down a long slide, and as she went down the slide monstrous things reached out and attacked her, hurting her terribly. In the dream it was important for her to be able to endure the tortures and get to the end of the slide because God was watching her.

The wrist continued giving her pain despite the treatments and the splint. Then a miraculous thing happened. Her wrist was healed.

The young pastor requested that she tell in church about her healing. She stood and told how she had been living with self-pity, feeling sorry for herself over her wrist. As she prayed God had made this inner attitude known to her, and in turn she asked forgiveness for it. As the forgiveness took place a great wave of heat flowed down her arm and into her wrist and hand. She was healed. The swelling subsided, and life eased up.

Chapter 9

The Never Ending Battle

"The battle belongs to the Lord"
(11 Chronicles 20:15)

Serum hepatitis struck Char again at age fourteen. She was very, very sick and spent most of her time sitting in a rocking chair in the living-room rocking and rocking and listening to classical music turned up loud on the stereo. Her diseases of diabetes and hemophilia complicated each other. She had to be on a low fat diet for the hepatitis and a low sugar diet for the diabetes, and so she lived on diet soda, crackers, and carrot sticks. Her bruising seemed more severe. She even had little bruises on her cheeks where her glasses rested.

I began to be frightened. She looked so sick and wasn't getting any better. I knew that the liver has to heal itself. It entered my head that she might die.

Over the weeks I tried to please her. When Char was ill or in pain, and especially if it was ruining her plans, she did not complain but she became angry. In the hospital she was a good patient, admired for her up-beat attitude and courage, but at home she could be cross and ugly - a miserable patient. Most of her hostility was aimed at me. Nothing I cooked suited her. Nothing I said encouraged her, she said that I didn't understand. None of my suggestions were followed. She didn't take care of herself real well, and became angry at me when I questioned her on the diabetes tests, etc.

One day I went shopping and searched very carefully to buy her some underwear that she would like. I brought it home to her. From her rocking chair she stuck up her nose. It wasn't the kind she liked. She didn't want it. At that point I exploded, yelling, "I don't care how sick you are, I'm a human being and I expect to be treated like one! You have no right to treat me like this." I slammed out the door. I made up my mind. I was not going to allow her to become a monster, no matter how sick she was. Even if she was sick enough to die.

Later, when I talked to my mother, she made an evaluation of Char's rejection of me and her rebelliousness. She said, "Char is so dependant upon you that if she doesn't break away she'll never be able to stand on her own two feet." It was hard for me to see this independent girl as dependant upon me, but my mother usually had the correct vantage point.

Years later I found that she had written in her journal:

I just don't know what's wrong with me. Mom is especially nice to me and I'm so mean back. I was just terrible. I feel really awful. I've just got to be nice. O God, please help me and guide me now so that I can be sincere, pure, and happy.

Something was wrong with the horse. "Heaves" they said. Heavy breathing. Lung problems. Lethargy. The tube worming had made her worse. The vet came, medication was given, and special feed, but it wasn't enough. Cindy died. How we all grieved for Char. Her wonderful dream. Her horse! Gone.

Char wrote in her journal:

Why God? She was going to get better. She shouldn't have died. There are so many horses, why her? O Cindy, Cindy. I feel so empty.

Several weeks after Cindy was buried in the horses' burial yard down by the creek, a ray of light began to shine again for Char. Our neighbors that owned the horse barns gave Char a little Morgan foal of theirs. He was a splendid 6 month old registered Morgan. She named him Sonny. And along with the foal came the offer to cover the cost of vet's bills, feed and other expenses. Now a whole new era opened up for Charmaine - training the horse, 4-H classes, showing horses herself, working with the hired man and other horse trainers. She worked hard every day, quietly sneaking out of the house at 5am.

Ron and I did not want her working so hard because often her physical body was weak or injured. But her spirit demanded this release.

Years later the hematologists found out that physical activity actually raised the factor 8 level in the body (the element she was missing). It showed up in the fact that Char often felt better after hard work.

Char learned to block out pain. Years later she wrote about it for a college writing class.

Hemophilia and I

The first thing that I remember is pain; everything hurt. When I was little, every time I bumped into a table or a chair, or crawled on my knees, or ran around, or

45

fell down, I got bruises. The bruises hurt when I moved, and I never failed to bump the same bruise over and over everyday, making it worse. Soaking in a warm tub at night, I would concentrate on counting all the bruises on each leg to see which one had the most. Usually, when I got past thirty on one leg, I'd lose count. I rarely did find out which had more.

I remember very clearly the first time I purposely blocked out pain. I was running through the dining room toward the bathroom, when I smashed into the dining room table. Pain seared through my arm, and I doubled over, gripping my shoulder. Then I realized that pain was part of me, like a small, persistent voice that would never go away, and that would forever try to break me. But I was strong, and I had a purpose, so I would win.

After that, any time I got hurt, I would pause for a split second to let the initial shock penetrate; then I'd ignore it. No matter how long the pain persisted or how much it interfered with what I was doing, I would not acknowledge it. Quite often my mother would spot an unusually big or gross bruise and ask me how I got it. My mind would whirl. I would flash back on everything I had done that day, but my mind would be blank: I had blocked it out too well.

As I got older, I started to develop severe joint bleeds. The only treatment at that time was to pack the joint in ice to try to slow the bleeding. With an elbow or an ankle immobilized in ice, I would be forced to sit for weeks, bearing never-ending pain. The only reason I survived was because God held me up.

Pain is part of my life, but I have always believed it has a purpose. Driving me to the ultimate limit of my endurance, pain seems to just be testing me, making me get stronger to survive this world. I never remember being told specifically about God; he just seemed to always be there.

But I love life. Through pain, God has shown me many things that I would otherwise been too obnoxious to notice. He's been able to stop me and make me look at my life, my personality, and my attitude toward other people. I'm able to see the best in bad situations and know that the Lord is there. I am able to look at other people and see God shining through them. Through his strength, I am able to conquer worldly "things." I have to everyday. I love life for God is here: I am living proof. He has blessed me more than abundantly.

Char continued to work very hard with Sonny. She won some prizes, but the biggest thrill of all was being awarded "Grand Champion" at Ludlow day. Wearing a new brown riding habit, sitting atop a new saddle which was purchased by her supportive aunt and uncle, we have a picture of a radiant Char.

Chapter 10

Adventures With Doc

"That every man may find satisfaction in all his toil --this is the gift of God."
(Ecclesiastes 3:13)

The neighbor, who lived on the other side of our house, was a veterinarian. When Char got into high school she began to work with him in her spare time. She would go over and help him during office hours in his clinic. Often they would go out to farms, Char tagging along to find out about the maladies for which cows are prone. Doc didn't spare her anything. He let her know about the "east end of a cow going west."

She told us about soaping her arm up to the shoulder and under Doc's instruction, reaching into a cow to turn a calf that stubbornly didn't want to be born.

Char wrote:

I stepped right up to the back-end of the cow and eased my arm in. The world I entered was incredible. Every sense flooded into my arm; I was seeing with my hand. Soft, buoyant warmth closed around my arm as I felt the pressure of the cow's uterine muscles contract. I could feel darkness; it seemed tangible. Almost immediately I felt the slippery smoothness of the calf's sac against his front feet.

I spread the loop of the chain out as best I could with my fingers and tried to slide it around one hoof, but the sac was too slippery and I couldn't maneuver it well enough to get it on. The calf, not appreciating having his quiet, secure world disturbed, started to slip back into the womb. I reached right after him as far as I could, but he was gone. Just as I was about to say something to Doc, the mother cow heaved. Her strong muscles squeezed my arm, almost cutting off the circulation, but the calf was back.

In the background I could her Doc talking to Frank, they seemed far away, remote; we were in different worlds.

With the cow's regular contractions keeping the calf in place, I finally slid a chain over each foot. My arm, bloody and slimy, felt like putty after fighting the strong muscle for such a long time, but the calf was ready to come out!

"It's about time you came out. I didn't know what you were doing. Though maybe you got lost in there!"

With a wink, Doc hooked a rope to the two chains and looped it around a supporting beam.

My stomach clenched when the baby hit the hard, concrete isle way. What a cruel way to start life after the soft security of his mother's womb. I couldn't believe that calves were just pushed out like that and allowed to hit the ground. But the calf didn't seem to be too phased, and after being dragged around to the mother's head, seemed quite content to be licked.

Char decided that as her life's work she wanted to be a veterinarian.

One time my sister wanted her cat, Boots, spayed but couldn't afford it, so Char talked with Doc about letting her do the operation. She had watched him so many times she was sure she could do it. My sister was willing to take the risk with the cat. The procedure was set up to be performed in Doc's clinic.

Char said that as Doc directed her with the operation he paced back and forth, puffing on one cigar after another like a nervous father. The operation proceeded OK, but a problem arose.

Doc had given the cat an extra dose of anesthetic to cover Char's surgical procedure, as he knew she would be slower. As a result, the cat didn't come out of the anesthetic at the right time.

Char worriedly carried Boots home, who looked very much like a dead cat. The cat's legs were stiffening out and it didn't look hopeful.

That night Char slept in a sleeping bag with Boots on her chest to keep her warm. Every time the cats leg's would stiffen up she'd exercise them, trying constantly to stroke Boots and bring her along.

In the wee hours of the morning the cat wet and began to stir. Much to all of our great relief, Boots made it!

Chapter 11

Home Transfusions

"For the Lord...will have compassion on his afflicted ones" (Isaiah 49:13)

The summer that Charmaine was 17, Todd 15, and Andrea 5, we decided, at the urging of the Hemophilia Center, to be trained in giving home transfusions. We had suffered through some bad experiences at the hospital when the nurses or technicians couldn't "get a vein," or when they insisted on using large gauge needles that would cause damage or scarring to the vein.

In learning to do our own transfusions we would , with practice, become the experts. We would use the tiny butterfly needles that would spare the veins. We would be trained in preparing the blood product, thawing etc, aseptic technique and recording the use of product as well as administering it. It would give us much more freedom. No more waiting in hospitals. No more long hours of driving, explanations, paper work etc. We would travel to Rochester twice a week for the next 6 weeks to learn the procedure.

But it wasn't easy to learn. Nobody likes to stick a needle, no matter how small, into their own vein. As a skill, it would take quite a few sticks to master it, Char and Todd made light of it to cover their nervousness, but five year old Andrea decided "No," and used the tactic of screaming at the top of her lungs to try and get out of it.

Since I was the one assigned to transfusing her, each session was nothing short of an ordeal.

Char wrote this about the adventure of learning to give home transfusions:

TRANSFUSIONS

Sitting in the Rochester Hemophilia Center treatment room at two, small tables facing each other, Todd and I were each equipped with a sterile blue pad, bountiful 2x2 gauze pads, alcohol swabs, quarter inch tape, a number 23 green butterfly needle, a tubing set up with ten bags of thawed blood product, and a tourniquet. This was it. Today we were going to give our own transfusions. All week we had been learning the sterile process of thawing and reconstituting our blood product, cryoprecipitate, and now we were anxiously waiting for George with his final instructions on "getting your vein, but not destroying it."

I glanced over at my brother. The size of the treatment room seemed to dwarf him. It was odd how a healthy, fifteen year old boy could appear so small and pale. He looked a little nervous but he had control of the situation. I knew he'd do fine and I prayed I would too.

Thinking back, I remembered all those years at the hospitals where the nurses just wouldn't seem to get my veins. Digging into my bruised hands and elbows, I would silently endure their savage 18 gages.

But always it would be the same and they would apologetically say as they missed a vein for the third time, "The vein was there. I don't know what happened, it just seemed to disappear." My stomach tightened in apprehension. I would be sticking needles into my own arm in just a few minutes.

"Hey Char, here, hold up your arm, let me get your vein." Then Todd, from ten feet across the room, skillfully pretended to throw a needle at me. I moved my exposed arm slightly to the right.

"Great job! You hit the big vein in the elbow but it was the wrong elbow!"

Laughingly I said, "Here, let me get the little vein in your left knee." The nervous tension that had been building up in both of us broke as we laughed and joked at our own absurdity. When the technician walked in, we slowly came back to reality, but we were both much more at ease.

The technician was talking, "Now you would mentally calculate the distance of the vein below the skin. Using about a 45° angle, you would stick the needle under the first layer of skin and with a definite, arc-like motion you would lower the angle of the needle and go in." George, strapping a tourniquet around his own brown arm was going to demonstrate the technique on himself!

With ease, he slipped the needle into an almost undistinguishable vein in his left elbow. Instantly, bright red blood flowed down the small plastic tube. My brother and I concentrated on every move that he made because our time was drawing near. As he jerked the needle out of his vein, George broke the silence with a smile, "Alright, now it's your turn. Any questions?"

"Yes, can we go home now?" Todd was being his usual self!

As I checked and unwrapped my small butterfly needle, I thought back to what the treatment had been like when I was small. It was amazing how the treatment for hemophiliacs had improved over the last few years. Whole blood transfusions had been given, but then only under extreme circumstances. Joint bleeds had to be packed in ice for months and the pain just endured. Now, concentrates, which could be taken every twelve hours, were given instead of blood; so joint bleeds were treated much more efficiently. The research that was being done by the Center's staff was incredible, and I was amazed that the Center could teach people how to treat themselves. Excitement flowed through me at the thought of independently transfusing myself, and I felt calm, almost at ease as I picked up the grey tourniquet and went for my left elbow.

It did make our lives easier and the treatment less of an ordeal. I learned how to give the transfusions at that time. Ron was eager to learn the procedure, and several years later when time would allow him, went to the Center to be trained.

A camaraderie developed among our children with hemophilia. Char wrote in a college English paper of an orthopedic appointment she shared with Andrea:

Sitting side by side on the treatment table, dressed in identical white cotton gowns, Andrea and I smirked at each other while the orthopedic doctor and three other specialists discussed our ankle x-rays.

I hadn't seen Andrea for over a month, and we sat, close together swinging our bare legs back and forth, as she eagerly whispered to me all about school and her second grade teacher.

When the doctor's conversation turned to her ankle, she stopped talking and tensed up.

"The contortion is worse and the bleeding hasn't stopped. I feel at this point that we should transfuse her three times a week." The doctor looked tired and his face was drawn as he gently rotated Andrea's feet around testing her range of motion.

Andrea's face contorted in an awkward smile and she let out a short sigh.

"Oh brother," her voice quivered as she looked down at her already used, sore veins, "that's my only good one."

"But Andrea," I leaned over, brushing shoulders with her, "Just think, with three transfusions a week you'll be super woman."

Andrea:
She always talked to me like an equal, not "talking down" to her baby sister. She would tell me what was happening to her and what it felt like.

****

Gloria:
I always thought that Char's hemophilia and experiences were kind of neat, because it was different. The home transfusions were cool. It was different than other people.

****

Mark:
The things I remember most about Char were her optimism and determination. Despite having such physically disabling diseases as hemophilia and diabetes, she trained and showed horses, raised all kinds of animals, and went on calls with a neighboring veterinarian.

****

Char continued to fall prey to all kinds of illnesses, yet she never seemed like a sick person. No one ever labeled her as sick, but rather as brave or courageous. When people came to visit her she would talk about her animals with enthusiasm. They would go away impressed.

In her Senior year in high school, nearing graduation, Char was leading an extremely busy life and suffering from a continuous, severe sore throat. I thought that she probably had Mono (Mononucleosis) and although the doctors said "No" to that diagnosis, I talked them into taking the test for it, and sure enough, it was.

One of Char's favorite brothers was Cal. A year and a half older than her, he had been very protective of her when they were little. In fact, if Char was bleeding or in pain as a preschooler, we immediately got Cal out of the room because it was so upsetting to him.

Now, as older brother, he was a great tease. Wadding a cloth around a spoon to look like a microphone, he mock interviewed Char. "Hello, I hear that you've had more diseases than anyone in the state. Let's see, you have hemophilia and diabetes, is that right? And you've had hepatitis twice, you say, and now mononucleosis. That's quite a prestigious accomplishment."

Although his teasing temporarily eased the tension, Charmaine sunk to a low. She later wrote this paper concerning this point in her life:

I NEEDED TO BE STOPPED

When I came down with mono during the last week of school during my senior year, I thought it was the worst thing that could happen to me; little did I realize that good that would come from it. Being a determined, strong-willed person, I have always had a full life, and the last month of school was no exception. Finals in physics, American studies, Calculus I, and English were quickly crashing down upon me. I was caught up in the thrill and awesomeness of assisting a veterinarian;

the excitement but fatiguing frustration of training a completely spoiled Doberman Pincher Puppy; and the serious responsibility of managing a Morgan horse farm, which was a major factor of my life. I was also playing the organ for church services, giving five piano lessons, and exercising Arabians with my horse trainers on weekends. Time was my enemy, for everything I had to do took time; my life was one long, head-on, mad rush, and on I rushed not taking the time to sort out priorities. I was centered on myself, always preoccupied with what I was going to do next, which horses I was going to work, when I was going to clean the barn, and walk the Doberman, and how I was going to get home on time for supper so my mother wouldn't be mad.

I was beginning to slip into the mode of consciously ignoring the fact that I was allowing my selfish priorities to become the most important things in my life, even more important than my family and other people. But my Father in heaven was wide awake and not oblivious to this fact. Three days before school was to end, I was diagnosed as having mononucleosis. Walking out of the hospital with my mother after we found out the blood test was positive for mono, I crumbled. Everything I was involved with and all my plans for the summer were instantly devastated, for I now faced at least three months of absolute rest. Oblivious to every sense, I walked across the parking lot to our car and slumped in. My whole body shook as I tried to suppress my tears. "Why, Oh Lord, Why? This can't be happening now. Why me? Why is there always something wrong? No God! No! No! No!" I cried and my mother cried with me. But then my pity hardened to bitterness.

I remained bitter and sunk into a shell for days, completely filled with inner turmoil. With mono, I was now confined to the house, and every form of physical work was restricted. I couldn't go back to school, I couldn't take my final exams, I couldn't train the Doberman, I couldn't work with the veterinarian, I couldn't give piano lessons or play the organ, and most unbearable of all I couldn't continue running the barns and riding or showing the horses.

The horses had filled every special place in my life for over six years, and my entire being wanted to rebel when I wasn't even allowed to go and see them. I wanted to hate what mono was doing to my life. I wanted to hate it so badly, but slowly I began to realize that there was some reason for this crisis to strike now, and I forced myself to face the truths that I had conveniently avoided for so long: I was so involved in me that I didn't even stop to look at what I was, or how I acted toward other people, or the fact that my attitude, especially toward my parents, really stunk. But suddenly, since mono had lifted every single responsibility from me, the only thing I had left was time; time to peer closely into myself and see what a mess I had been heading for.

I sat in the living room rocking chair,

huddled in an old blanket like a wounded animal, rocking back and forth thinking about my life. I saw with horror what an uncaring person I was beginning to turn into, and how my attitude toward my family was fast becoming extremely obnoxious and snide. I was shocked. I had always thought of myself as a very open, pleasant, and sincere individual, always thoughtful and sympathetic, ready to make immediate sacrifices in order to help someone else. But rocking in the corner, isolated by mono, and watching the close interactions of my family, I was jarred into the reality that my life was seriously contradicting all the preconceived, good ideas of what I thought I was. I realized that with mono, God was making me stop and evaluate myself. I was ashamed and humbled to think that I had been so utterly in tune with myself and out of tune with God, that the only way he could reach me was by literally stopping my physical body. I saw that I had wrapped my life and all my emotions up with the horses, thus blocking out all other concerns and alienating myself from my family. And I saw that I terribly resented my parents whenever they tried to limit my activities or slow me down.

But this was wrong because I really did love my parents and family very dearly, and I knew deep inside I was really a good person. So I sincerely prayed to God, and he helped me change my priorities and enlighten my attitude. God, once again, became first in my life,

letting all my hidden, good feelings flow
once more. And one morning:

I arose to watch a sunrise
Eager to see the sky
Something I had not often done
For Time flew too quickly by

As wondrous glories of color
Merged in the lightening dawn
The power and Glory of God
Was revealed in majestic song

The peace and courage that came to me
As I gazed at the broadening sky
Made my heart within me
Praise the One most High

The importance of good-will and joy
Radiating to all from my heart
Was a lesson I learned through trials that stopped me
And showed me how to begin a new start

We had all hoped that Charmaine would be well enough to attend her high school graduation. Seeing her walk up the aisle to Pomp and Circumstance and cross the stage to receive her diploma, NY State Regents Scholarship and music awards was a thrill for all of us.

Some of Char's recuperation was spent at her grandmother's house. Her grandmother was a special person to Char. And wouldn't you know it, they found an abandoned baby skunk, which Char took into the house, and kept in a shoe box, bathing and feeding and nurturing. It seemed that God always sent an animal to Char. Wherever she went they were put in her path. Maybe these were angels in disguise. They certainly took the role of uplifting and restoring her.

Chapter 12

Up, Up, And Away

"There is a time for everything, and a season for every activity under heaven"
(Ecclesiastes 3:1)

Char was going to be leaving home in the fall to attend college. She would be recovering from mononucleosis during the summer and then leaving her familiar surroundings. She would be taking the next step of being on her own. Her mind was in a quandary about what to do with her horse, Sonny, when she went to college. She didn't want to just "let him rot." Without daily workouts, grooming and training, he would lose his progress as a Morgan show horse and be relegated to the pasture. Char couldn't bear the thoughts of that. Although Gloria had often been her partner at the barn, and had helped with working the horses, Gloria was not interested in doing it alone. She was becoming more interested in excelling at the piano and couldn't devote the time to it.

Heartbreaking as it was, Char decided she must sell Sonny. She wanted him to progress and four years of college plus fours years of expected vet school was too long to keep him waiting.

A young man was interested in Sonny and came to try him out. He rode him around the ring recklessly. He wanted to buy him but didn't come back with the money, which was a relief as Char was unhappy with his treatment of the horse.

Finally a family came with a twelve year old daughter who really took to Sonny. It seemed that she was the one. Hard as it was to see Sonny go, we were glad that he went to a new, good mistress.

In the fall of 1979, Char started college at Houghton, majoring in Pre-Med. / Science.

Although still tired and struggling to overcome the mono, she was eager to start.

Char had a great time at college. She did very well in English classes, where she wrote up all the stories of her animals and her adventures with Doc. She kept up writing in her journal, pouring her heart out on its pages, especially over a young man she had met and was dating.

In high school she had gone to a few proms but never really dated anyone. She seemed to be too deep and serious for the boys her age. But now, in college, her sparkle and love of life made her more appealing to the guys. Although she dated this young man, by the end of the school year it had faded.

Char was a good student because she was very determined and worked very hard.

At the end of her Freshman year at college she had the opportunity to go to Brazil with Augusta, an exchange student who had been living with us for the school year. They had become friends when Char had come home for holidays and occasional weekends.

If she could get the money for air fare, her stay there would be free as Augusta was from a wealthy family. The money had come in from the sale of the horse, so it was decided she should go. We felt that it was the chance of a lifetime!

People questioned us on letting her go so far away. I was confident that as God took care of her here, He would also take care of her there. So, packing an extra case with insulin for the diabetes, and a new concentrate (not necessary to deep freeze) for the hemophilia, off she went.

Charmaine loved Brazil; its sights, its sounds, especially its ambiance; a relaxed and friendly atmosphere. It was a different world, and one in which she felt at home. Adventures awaited her at every turn.

There were adventures with food. She experienced going to the open market with her host mother (mamae).

Char wrote in her journal:

Lunch is the biggest meal of the day in Brazil and sitting at the big heavy wooden dining room table, I looked over at my Brazilian mother; Mamae. Her lips were pressed tightly together. She was never happy at meals because she thought I didn't eat enough. The rest of the family, Fatima, Marcelo, Augusta, and Pae, all "out-ate" me by about four times – each.

"Your Mother will spank you when you go home because you will be too thin," mamae said in Portuguese while going through the motions of being spanked.

"No, she'll spank me because I'll be too fat! I eat too much," I joked in broken Portuguese, Mae smiled but I knew she wasn't any happier.

My family and everyone else I met in Brazil, no matter how heavy or thin ate enormous amounts of rice, spaghetti, macaroni, brown beans, potatoes and bread. They didn't eat green vegetables, except occasionally cabbage cooked in a sauce, and they served 2 or 3 kinds of meat at every lunch. The little loaves of French style bread were brought in early every morning fresh from a bakery, and all the fruit, oranges, pineapple, cocoa-nuts, bananas and melons were freshly picked. Nothing was bought in cans or mixes, it was all natural and homemade.

After my first few days in Brazil, I slowly began adjusting to their food and spices. I could only eat small amounts of rice and black beans because they were so filling. Mae took it as my not liking them so everyday she fixed different things for me. When she found something I liked it was if she'd made a major breakthrough. I'd find a special little dish of it setting next to my plate for the next three weeks.

When the meat, especially beef was served, I could never tell exactly what it was or what part of the animal it came from.

I'd say, "Augusta, what is this?" Looking at a lump of ominous dark meat sitting in a pool of oil. "Just try some. It's good." Augusta had lived at my house in New York for 6 months and knew English. She was a year younger than me. "No. Tell me what it is first, then I'll try some. Come on Augusta, What is it?"

"No, try some. Here, experiment. Experimenter."

She would never tell me what kind of meat it was. Everything was "experimenter, experimenter! It's good." But I couldn't stomach the thought of possibly eating cow brain or lung or some other unknown parts, so I usually didn't eat any beef at all. I mostly lived on eggs, fried chicken, spaghetti, and fresh fruit because I could identify it.

Every Friday morning at six o'clock, Augusta, Mae, and I would go to the open market to buy the week's supply of fruit, vegetables and meat. The market was set up in a dirty, grungy, narrow street with crude wooden stands crowded along each side. Old or rotten fruit was thrown into the street only to be stepped on and mushed by all the passing donkeys and carts that were loaded down with "goods."

Every week, the same small, sturdy man with a worn brown leather hat would meet mamae as she entered the street and carry her huge woven basket on his head. We'd walk up the street, stopping where the fruits looked especially good.

Each stand had a primitive type balance, and Mae would pick through the vegetables, piling the good ones on one side of the balance while the seller put little weights on the other. Then Mae would put the potatoes, tomatoes, melons, pineapple, coconut, oranges, carrots, or onions, flour and dried beans into the basket and move on. By the time we finished the basket would be so heavy that it would take one other man to help Jaoa heave it over his head and steady it as he straddled beneath, adjusting his position. His neck muscles would bulge under the strain but he'd follow mae dodging in and out among the people and animals with ease.

By the time mae was done with the fruits, the sun would be just beginning to blaze over the store roof tops. Even though it was their winter, it was rarely under 70°F.

In the street there weren't too many flies because this was their "cold" season and flies didn't like the cold, but in the meat building it was like stepping into fly heaven.

The concrete meat building had a high roof, no lights and many open door ways. Men with Samurai-shaped knives, stood at old wooden benches hacking away at fly-covered carcasses while scrubby dogs, every size and description, most with mange, ran in and out snatching up scraps of meat that fell to the floor. The floor was wet, and a heavy stench hung in the warm, humid air making it almost impossible to breath. This was in the early morning even before the sun was fully up or the heat of the day had set in, and there was no refrigeration anywhere.

Mae would stop at one of the many little booths setup across the floor, select a piece of meat, and wait while it was cut and wrapped. The brown wrapping paper had about the consistency of paper towels and blood from the meat would immediately soak through making it a nice mess for Augusta and I to carry back to the car. With the open market buying done, mae would then go to a "Market Basket" to finish buying meat.

The Market Basket had no refrigerated sections, and the unwrapped meat, either salted or sun dried, was piled in stacks in the back of the store. I could smell it before we got half way back, but mae would go right in and forcibly pull out a piece from the middle of the stack. After smelling it all over and deciding it was "fresh" she'd buy it. I thought it looked like shriveled shoe leather.

After my first market day with mae and Augusta, I didn't seem to have much of an appetite for beef, but the chicken, which we bought at a nice little chicken shop, looked safe enough and was very good. Nenem, the domestic servant who cooked every meal, would serve chicken two ways. It was either fried or cooked in a sauce and served in a casserole dish. I always ate the fried chicken, but one day I decided to make a special effort to please mae.

"Mae, passa a gallinha por favor."

Mamai's face it up and she eagerly passed the casserole style chicken to me. The sauce was red and oily but the chicken looked normal so I reached right in and scooped out a small breast piece. I was glad that Mae was so happy. I knew how nervous mae had been about having an American.

"Maybe I should start trying more things just to please her," I thought to myself as I put the spoon back in the bowl. But my thought was cut short, for there, neatly garnishing each side of the dish, laid two large, protruding chicken legs - complete with scales, claws and toe nails.

Char had adventures with the culture – maids and servants did much of the household work, and were included in the family in watching television at night.

Adventures in the language – learning Portuguese and laughing at the mistakes and pranks pulled on her through language.

Adventures in romance. Char had never thought herself a pretty girl. But with blue eyes and light brown hair she was looked upon as a beauty by Augusta's circle of friends. She met, and dated , and fell in love with a young man named Cacai.

She visited him where he worked; at a School for Special Children.

In her journal she wrote:

My whole heart went out to those children. It's such a special kind of work. I really want to work there the rest of the time I'm here. I don't want to be paid. I'd just like to help.

After I saw the whole school I sat in Cacai's office and talked with him. He asked me what I'd do if we fell in love -- had I thought about it? I said that when I finished college I'd move to Brazil. Our conversation ended with the question "What are we going to do for the next six years with me in college in the USA and Cacai here in Brazil? I don't know. I just don't know.

My whole being moves out toward Cacai, but I never can seem to express my true feelings when I'm with him. It's such a hard thing to have to decide between home and Brazil and Cacai. Dear God, Please help me.

When she returned home she brought his picture and a longing to return to Brazil.

The end of the summer was at hand and Char transferred to Cornell University. A place had opened up for her there, and since she hoped to attend their College of Veterinary Medicine, she thought she would have a better chance of getting accepted if she finished her undergraduate work there.

Going from a small Christian college to a huge Ivy League school was a shock for Charmaine. Her single room was a tiny one, located at the end of a long hall in an antiquated dorm, The only thing that kept her afloat that year was the presence of her two parakeets.

She was shocked to find that a new friend in college regularly had abortions. And a girl next door hired a guy to write all her papers and cheated on her exams. This was exposure to a different kind of world for her.

Pain in her left wrist, her writing hand, made much of the work difficult. She began to attend the various campus ministries, looking for some kindred souls. She called home telling us that she had found a great group of dedicated Christians in a group called The Way. She wanted to take some intensive classes for it, which were rather expensive, but she explained that the cost would make sure that members made the commitment to the ministry. We hadn't heard of the group but guessed it was OK since she was so enthusiastic that she had found a Christian group to her liking.

Little did we know that it was considered a cult and would make great demands on her. However, in all fairness, it seemed to be what she needed. The group met every day and prayed for each other. The teaching focus was on the abundant life that Christ wanted for us, and that was ours. With the enormous load Char carried, with her health difficulties and college studies, the teachings kept her buoyed up and thinking positively.

We began to read some very negative things about The Way and it's control over its members, who all seemed to be college students and young adults in their twenties.

A friend of Char's who had joined the group was "rescued" by her parents, who snatched her home and sent her away to be deprogrammed.

Char wrote:

Heidi gave me this journal before we left Cornell. She made it. We were going to exchange them to read. Now, all that I can do is fervently lift Heidi and believe that she'll get her head together and get out of her situation. No matter what the "de-programmers" say about The Way - if she just gets quiet and listens to God, he'll show her the way. I hope that at the end of summer we'll be able to still share with each other.

(That never happened. She never saw Heidi again.)
We voiced our concern about this group to Char and she agreed to visit a young pastor she knew who ran a Youth For Christ group in our area. We went with her to the visit and discussed her involvement with "The Way" ministry and our concerns.

The pastor warned Char of some of the pitfalls and also told her of his experience with young people in the group; specifically that they were going into bars with their Bibles to testify, and staggering out drunk.

After the meeting we talked with the pastor, and he stated that he considered Char to be an "eclectic"; one who was picking up what she needed from the teaching and discarding the rest. He did not see it as extremely dangerous for her as she was grounded in the faith, and her basic beliefs hadn't changed. He had cautioned her to be wary of what would be fanatical teachings of the group.

Regardless of how we felt about that group, those students were major supportive friends in the days that were to come.

Char returned to Brazil the next summer, in opposition to our strong advice against it. We thought that it was too costly, and her money should go toward college. But she worked for her aunt for the money and borrowed the rest. We reluctantly took her to the airport and put her on the plane. In Brazil, Char was able to work with some veterinarians.

She wrote in her journal:

July 2, Friday
This will be my third day working with a Veterinarian here in

Caruaru. He is absolutely amazing with animals and I don't think I've ever learned this much in as short a time and had such a wonderful time doing it. Armindo, whose parents sell shoes from a van, talked with a vet he knew on Monday, and on Tuesday he took me on his motorcycle to where the vet was going to operate on a cow. The cow's vulva was all ripped up. He injected novocaine all around it and cut out all the proud flesh – then sewed it up. He let me feel it - it looked excellent when he finished!

The next day, Wednesday, Armindo took me to the Pharmacia at 3:00 and we went way out in the mountains to some farms and vaccinated 110 cows, 4 goats and 2 horses conatra Raiva. They run the cows through a chute and then we vaccinated with a injection gun. He let me do almost all of them! Then Jose had to lasso a couple cows, he was amazing, and is going to teach me how to do it! Oh, so much happens everyday that it's hard to write about it. Later at another farm I saw a cow with rabies. They have a problem around here with rabies because they have a lot of blood -sucking bats. At this farm, Jose wanted me to go talk English with the cowboy. It was so funny to see his face because he couldn't understand ..nada. I really like the vet; he's the kind of person you immediately admire. I got home at one and returned to the clinic at 2:00pm. There was a dog there that was all swollen up from his head to almost his tail. When Jose lanced it, air went whoosh out and at the same instant he died. It could have been his heart, or maybe an air sac had leaked out under the skin and when he lanced it the inside pressure collapsed. Then we vaccinated 10 more cows.

It's beyond me how they raise crops here. There are no tractors anywhere and I see plots of corn way up the sides of mountains which must be planted by hand and harvested by hand. All the cows are rounded up either by foot or by cowboys on horses. At one farm I saw the saddles in the barn, they're hand tooled, and I've never seen such beautiful leather. I can't wait to ride a horse here.

Char had hoped to deepen her relationship with Cacai. She wrote:

I've had two serious discussions with Cacai. In the first, Cacai said that one time he loved a girl and she really ripped his heart. He gave so much of himself and now he has deep scars. He likes me very much and could love me, but he still hurts. I understood exactly how he felt, but it is so frustrating when there is such a language barrier.

June 30

The big thing that's on my heart is Cacai. At all the Sao Joao and Sao Pedro festas, and at Lima's party and at the Quadrilha he just about completely ignored me and lost himself amongst a lot of other girls.

After the first night of Sao Joao when he danced with everyone except me, I had Augusta call him so I could talk.

It seemed like he would ignore me every time he saw me. I knew it was because I liked him more than he liked me.

I've forced myself to be calm about him and I've been getting strength and peace from God. I'm telling myself that I'm slowly falling out of love.

In June I was tired all the time and slept most of the day. I was breaking out in bruises all over for no apparent reason. My eye swelled up twice and I had to give transfusions for it. I'd break out in a cold sweat every time I'd look at it and thoughts -- black thoughts of going blind filled my mind.

When things were going bad with Cacai and me it was hard to show my love for other people and hard to concentrate on the Portuguese language.

But God hasn't given up on me yet. The week of Sao Joao, the 20th of June, I received an absolutely beautiful letter from Grandma. She wrote a tribute to me. It really touched my heart. After reading her letter I immediately went to God's word, and started feeling much better about life. Then, Sat. the 27th, I received a letter from Lynn. My eye was threatening to act up again and panic was rising inside, but God graciously worked through her to touch me. She was strong on Positive Believing and that pulled me back to Praising the Lord and I was blessed with Romans 12:2 "And be not conformed to this world; but be ye transformed by the renewing of your mind that ye may prove what is that good, and acceptable, and perfect, will of God!"

Ever since then I've been excited with life again and I've been able to calm my anguish for Cacai!

Char began to focus on other things.

Her adventures in Brazil included a new pet. She wrote:

We stopped at a "Hipi" table on the street where a guy was making and selling metal jewelry. I noticed a tiny animal tied to the leg of the table. That's when I met "Jeiro" and fell in love with him! I bought Jeiro for 500 cruzeiros from the guy's girlfriend and we went home.

Jeiro is a Saguin; I think a type of monkey. He's tiny and can sit in the palm of your hand with plenty of room. He loves bananas, and will also eat canjica, laranjas, bolo and candy. He was pretty agitated the first night and was really dirty. The shoelace that was tied around his lower waist was cutting into him so Fatima and I made a new leash for him out of green yarn.

The first 2 days he only slept, ate, and went to the bathroom. Everyday he likes me more and is cleaner and has more energy. Every time , as soon as he wakes up, he has to go to the bathroom, so I rush him right out to the porch and let him go on a newspaper. I really hope I'll be able to "paper train" him.

I feed him off my finger and he's starting to get used to looking for me. On Sunday I was sitting on the porch wall when all of a sudden Jeiro became really agitated and jumped upon my shoulder. I looked all around to see what frightened him and directly under us, on the other side of the wall, was a cat, ready to jump! At least Jeiro considers me his protector.

She wrote of a visit to a farm:

I went with Joel and his mother, Lucinete, to their Fazenda. They've had it for 25 years. A man and his wife and 3 little daughters live there and take care of the land and 26 cows. They don't have electricity. The man was one of the happiest people I've seen. When he talked, he seemed excited about everything. He had a beautiful smile and twinkly eyes, and almost no teeth.

There were sunflowers, corn, beans and cacti. They took big pieces of cacti and ground them up in a machine. Joel gave me a piece to try. Little did I know that it was for the calves, so I took a big bite! We all laughed a lot especially me and then I went outside and spit it out!

We called in the 26 cows, bull and calves. We stood on a steep slope that slid down to a river below out of which another mountain arose on the other side. The cows, some with bells, slowly ambled up a path as the man called them. The land looks so different from anything I've ever seen before. It's like being on a different planet.

I was amazed at how they milk their cows. The man ran along behind a cow and with a rope tied her hind legs together. Then he lassoed the calf and tied its head to the mother's front leg. And there in the middle of the field he milked the cow by hand.

The little girls were pretty, but they had big pot-bellied stomachs. It doesn't look like malnutrition, but it may be because they eat mainly rice and black beans. There was a huge rock in back of the house and in a deep pool cut in the middle of it was a bright green mire, I imagine that it was sewage, seeing that they didn't have electricity.

A problem arose when Char prepared to come home to the U.S. because she wanted to bring Jeiro home with her, but transporting an animal out of the country was illegal. It would take extensive legalities to get him out as a household pet and would probably not be possible. Unknown to us, Char decided to smuggle him home on the plane with her. She prayed about the situation, made a pouch to carry Jeiro under a light jacket, got tranquilizer serum from the vet, and boarded the plane for the long flight to the U.S.

Things did not go well. Jeiro reacted to the tranquilizer with increased energy and agitation, rather than sleepiness. When he became noisy and the plane guards began to look around, she quickly went into the rest room and gave him another dose, and finally another. At last he was quiet, but to her heartache, had succumbed from the overdose.

When she arrived home she looked unhappy and stressed out. She buried Jerio in the back yard. She had prayed for Jerio to live, but God in His wisdom said, "No." Had she been apprehended illegally transporting an animal to another country, she would have been charged with a felony and banned from ever working with animals again. Her chance for vet school and fulfilling her lifelong dream would have been dashed.

It seems that God in His wisdom and mercy answers "No" to his foolish and stubborn children, to protect us from what would be the grievous results of our misguided decisions.

After another year at Cornell, Char worked for her aunt Bette again typing papers and doing housework to again earn money for a third return to Brazil.

She wrote about her time with her aunt:

Life is filled with so many pleasures and beauty. As I sit here and write, the woods are filled with the voices of birds enjoying the setting sun. My aunt's home is beautiful and is surrounded by trees, tall and stately, like angels guarding and keeping us as we live from day to day.

Upon returning to Brazil, Char intended to work with a couple in The Way ministry there. Having taken Portuguese at Cornell, she now spoke the language very well. To be a part of this ministry she had to find a job, but despite her language skills was unable to find one, so returned to the family of Marcelo and Augusta.

When she came home from this third trip we hoped that she had gotten Brazil out of her system -- at least the desire for any more trips there.

Upon her return we noticed that Char had developed some strange looking brown sore spots on her arms, legs, and feet that didn't heal up. We wondered if she had picked up some tropical skin disease from Brazil.

Char went back to college. She was not as big a part of our lives as she had been, but she wrote a lot and would burst in on holidays and enjoy her brothers and sisters, and then be off again.

She graduated from Cornell University in the spring of '83 with a degree in Agriculture and Life Science. After graduation her big aim was vet school; specifically the Cornell University School of Veterinary Medicine. That school had over a thousand applicants, out of which about eighty were chosen to attend.

Char prayed like mad. She believed that God wanted her to be a vet, and that she would get into the vet school. Although her grades were on the bottom side for acceptance, her enthusiasm and experiences in Brazil working with vets were a plus. The final interview went well, and she received the news that she was "in." What a joy that was for all of us. That fall she entered the vet school bright-eyed and bushy-tailed and in good health for her.

Chapter 13

Return To Battle

"...the devil left him until an opportune time" (Luke4:13).

I wish that I could end the story here and say that Char "lived happily ever after." Of course in God's perspective she did, but He had much more for her to accomplish here on this earth. And suffering seemed to be a part of it. The little plaque she gave me said it all: "I consider that the sufferings of this present time are not to be compared to the glory that will be revealed in us" (Ro. 8:18).

By this time, over eight years had gone by since I first started that one college course. I had continued attending college, adding more courses as the children grew older. After God touched my life in that life-changing experience, I had changed my major from Sociology to Theology and then to Religion. I had also changed colleges, and graduated with a BA in Religion from Houghton College in January, 1984.

I had spend six years filling the pulpit as a supply preacher, here and there, as the need arose. Now I was given the chance to candidate as pastor of a church. I was accepted by Ellisburg Union Church, in PA. I would commute there three days a week.

When the news arrived, I was in seventh heaven, praising God and leaping around. It was a beautiful day, the first real warm, breezy day in the spring. It was also the very day of the ninth anniversary of the wonderful experience I had had when God touched my life and became real to me. It was also the day after our little lost Robin's birthday. Often special things seemed to happen to me at that time.

But later in the day, as if Satan were attacking, we got a call from Char's friend at the hospital in Ithaca. Char had been out at a farm feeding her horse. (Yes, she had acquired another horse). A sheep on the farm, for some unknown reason, had rammed her in the knee, smashing it. She had been treated at the hospital there and they were sending her on to the Rochester General Hospital for more treatment.

It was quite a heroic story. Char had been at the barn alone when the accident happened. Not able to put any weight on that leg, and having to get up to a higher level in the barn, she sat down and dragged herself up the stairs to the next level and then a distance to the car. Struggling to get into the car, she managed to drive to her apartment, but no one was there to answer her frantic pounding on the horn. She then drove to a neighbor's and laid on the horn until someone came out to help her.

At the Rochester hospital she had to have a knee operation. Although the blood product kicked in to help control the internal bleeding, it was never 100% efficient, so she suffered more swelling, pain and more difficult recovery.

Complications set in. She got pneumonia. Since her recovery was so long, the doctors wondered if she could have contacted Legionnaire's disease, but that was ruled out and they decided the pneumonia was from the anesthetic.

Finally, she got well enough to come home on crutches, but she was still very sick. She was having some trouble bleeding from the bowel area, which was able to be partially controlled with the home transfusions.

Char insisted on going back to the vet school to try and make arrangements to make up her missed course work and finish out the semester. But she was too weak and ill and had to come home.

Bleeding from the bowel continued to give her more trouble, creating constant, terrible pain and diarrhea. One night the bleeding became severe, so we called for an ambulance to take her to Rochester. I climbed in the back with her and we sped off, siren screeching.

Suddenly I was jolted into the memory of riding in a speeding ambulance with baby Robin those many years before. Fear overtook me, but I had learned to be calm and detach myself and pray with trust, so now I released Char safely into God's hands.

Looking at her, I felt the presence of Jesus sitting at her side. Her pain stopped. All was quiet until we reached the outskirts of the city. The siren went on again. The excruciating pain came back, and the presence of Jesus was gone. Arriving at the emergency room in the middle of the night was a bad scene. Doctors on call did not understand her condition. They did give her a transfusion, but basically put her on hold until morning, not wanting to give her much pain-killer to mask the symptoms.

So she just had to gut it out, hour after weary hour, watching the clock tick, getting weaker by the moment.

A young woman who had attempted suicide by overdosing was brought in and put in the next cubicle. Nurses were pumping her stomach. I couldn't help but think, "One fighting to keep her life, and the other one in such despair as to try and end her life." How difficult a time it was. What were we all supposed to be learning?

More tests were taken, and a laser treatment was given Char in another hospital, but all to no avail. Doctors couldn't figure out what was causing the bleeding. Finally, they decided that an operation was necessary to find the cause.

Once again Ron and I sat in the hospital waiting room hour after hour, praying, praying, praying. My prayer scripture for her was always, "… in all things God works for the good of those who love him, who have been called according to his purpose." (Romans 8:28)

The surgery showed up a very unusual fungus infection; histoplasmosis. It had invaded her body. A section of her bowel was removed, and several lymph nodes. The surgeon found an unusual condition. He had never seen anything like it. He puzzled over it.

Char had to undergo chemotherapy to kill the fungus. She was in the hospital from the end of July until October. Her big concern was Cornell and her position in the vet school.

God is so good. In tragedy he sends out a lifeline. Dr. Lowe from the vet school arrived at the hospital with a big teddy bear for Charmaine and the comforting, restoring news that there would be a place for her at school. No matter how long it took her to get well, a place would be open. She could return and start over if she wanted.

Light shown in her eyes. Now, she was not a critically ill human being, she was, indeed, a student at the School of Veterinary Medicine, temporarily on leave of absence.

Her identity was strengthened.

When the young medical students came in to study her case or take tests, she collaborated with them as a student, and discussed her case with them. The doctors made her a part of the team in deciding upon her treatment. She talked knowledgeably with them.

For me, it was very difficult to hear these medical discussions repeated over and over. Eventually I learned to leave the room for a break at that time.

While she was in the hospital Char learned how to draw. She received many cards with animals on them, and she began to sketch the animals in large size on paper. She found that she could make an almost perfect likeness.

She told me, "Mom, I could never draw before. During that operation God opened up something in my mind that enabled me to draw!"

The doctors and nurses got very interested in Char's drawings and would bring in requests for pictures. One of her hematologists was so delighted with her drawing that he took the one she had made for him and had it matted and framed and put in his office.

A nurse told her, "Well, if you can do that, as sick as you are, I guess that I can do a few more things."

A student in the lab on the night shift would come up on her break and talk with Char. Friends from The Way came and held Bible studies with her.

Her best friend Monica from the vet school sent up a big box with a stuffed horse and cards from all the vet students. It kept her going. She was temporarily "on hold."

Ron and I took turns driving up to see her. On Sunday we would drive the hour south to the church where I was pastoring. Then we'd go back home to rest. Later, I would drive to Rochester to be with Char until Tuesday night.

Then Thursday or Friday, Ron would get off from school. The administration allowed him to take some of his accumulated sick days to visit her.

When she was really bad I would go back again later in the week.

One day, when she seemed to be "out" because of the heavy pain medication, I sat by her bed and read her the book of John. Later she remembered it.

The Lord sustained me through all of this. When I sat down to prepare a sermon for church, the thoughts would come so fast that I could hardly write them down quickly enough.

My two sisters, living in Rochester, opened their homes to us to stay overnight the many times Ron and I needed to.

Between trips to the hospital, I was able to keep up my church work. It was good for me and took my mind temporarily off Char's troubles.

Three months after she entered, Char was finally released from the hospital. She went to stay with her aunt Bette, who lived in a suburb, so that she could drive back and forth to the hospital three times a week to receive the chemotherapy. This was to be given for six months.

She had always liked her "benefactor" aunt and enjoyed staying there. During her time there she drew pictures to give to family members for Christmas presents.

She gave me a mother lioness with two cubs.

To her father, who was an avid hunter, Char gave a proud eight point buck.

For her aunt, there was a tiger. And for another aunt, there was a big-eyed owl.

Char decided to do some of the things she'd always wanted to do. We got a guitar for her combination birthday / Christmas present, and she arranged to take a few guitar lessons. Often we would hear the pleasant strum of the guitar when we went to visit.

At last the chemotherapy was over, and Char came home.

To be reduced to being a dependant family member again was distasteful to her. We gave her the largest upstairs bedroom, with a long, low bookcase as a room divider, so her room could seem more like a sitting room apartment.

I suggested she focus on training her horse, now housed in a neighbor's barn down the road. She put her mind to that.

The pain and diarrhea persisted, with weight loss, but worst of all, she began losing her eyesight.

I prayed continually for Char's healing. And many people prevailed in prayer for her from many churches in the U.S. and even Canada. I had prayed and fasted that she might be able to eat. She had lost so much weight and weighed less than a hundred pounds.

One day when I was driving up over the back hill on the way to work at the church, a voice spoke gently into my mind, inquiring of me, "Can you not pray for healing?"

It was then that I realized that she probably wasn't going to live.

God was telling me not to pray for healing.

I wept.

I changed my prayer for her that God's will would be done.

That Sunday I was to give communion at church for the first time. I prayed very hard ahead of time and worked hard to remember all the words. It was a very special time for me.

As I went to serve the bread as the body of Christ, and I spoke the words, "The body of our Lord Jesus Christ which was given for you," the inner voice of the Lord said very gently to me, "Can you give her up?"

God never asks us for anything unless He has prepared out hearts for it first. I was ready and answered, "Yes, God, I can give her up."

It was for me a real sacrament. I felt very close to God, who gave up His only son.

Chapter 14

He Makes No Mistakes

"God intended it for good to accomplish what is now being done"
(Gen. 50:20)

It was the week before Easter -- Holy Week -- and a week of strange happenings for us. Char had been admitted to the hospital after an overnight trial in the emergency room.

Ron and I trace the strange happenings back to a day a young nurse gave Char her pain medication via her Hickman line; a catheter to her heart. This was the routine way to give the medication, but the nurse gave it very fast.

Ron, who was at her bedside that day, said that immediately following the injection Char sat straight up in bed and then fell back convulsing. Her heart stopped beating. The nurses went into action, shocking her heart to get it going again. They were able to get it beating again and she came around.

After that, every several hours her whole body would jump, as if she were given an electric shock. It always startled her and she remarked on it.

This experience became more frequent. Then Char became very restless and started a stream of continuous talking. It seemed like a nervous disorder.

A nurse shooed the relatives out of the room, drew the curtains and tried to settle her down, to no avail.

Then Char's mind began to ramble and her talking did not make sense. It was as if someone were flipping the pages of an encyclopedia very rapidly.

Char talked continuously in a rather pleasant sing-song voice, reeling off information about crustaceans under the sea. (She could see their faces).

"Dr. Olson is talking to a rhododendron," she said. "Whales communicate forever."

On and on she talked. I wondered if her body would give out from exhaustion.

Sometimes we laughed. What she said was so funny. Sometimes I cried to see her so out of her mind.

Everything was extremely speeded up for Char. She picked up on every minute thing that was going on in the room and remarked on it. Her ears and eyes seemed acutely sensitive.

She talked about the airplane flying overhead and the noise of the traffic outside and when doors were opening and closing and when people were coming down the hall outside her room and who they were (Amazingly, she was correct!)

"Cal is here. He's coming down the hall." (He was!)

She picked up on when we blinked our eyes or shrugged or sat down or got up or glanced out the window. All in a sing-song voice.

"Mom is laughing. Dr Olson blinked his eyes."

A continuous running soliloquy.

At times she was annoyed with me.

"Mom stop talking on the telephone. You're using up everyone's oxygen."

Many other serious medical problems were happening. She had to go into the ICU and have continuous oxygen. She was still talking continuously, picking up on everything that was being said about all the people in all the cubicles around her.

She told the lab technician, who drew her blood, that he was Satan.

She began to get very focused on Satan and insisted that all the medical processes that were being done to her were Satanic.

Char seemed to be totally out of her head, yet she could answer rational questions. A member of the medical/neurology team asked her about his tie. She indicated which way the stripe went. (Strange, because her eyesight was failing, yet during this time she could see acutely.)

She was taken out of ICU and back to her room.

She began to see all of us, first as evil, then as good. She chided me about it.

"Mom, you're doing it again," she said in an annoyed voice.

Some people, even family, she decided were evil and told them about it. She was adamant about not wanting them in the room.

Chapter 15

Evil Enters.

"...the devil prowls around like a roaring lion looking for someone to devour"
(I Peter 5:8)

It was night, and I felt that Char was getting worse. She was now semi-conscious because of the heavy doses of morphine which had been given to her for pain. Her body was swelling and she looked bad.

I was getting exhausted from my bedside watch, which I deemed was necessary. Since Char had been "out," I prayed night and day for her. I somehow felt protective of her soul, since she seemed to be separated from all her spiritual strength and fight. Her condition was perilous.

Even though, by the power of my will I had let go of Charmaine, and put her directly into the hands of God, accepting his answer, still my human instincts were to help my daughter in need.

I had told God that I "let go." But until He let me know distinctly that her death was immanent I would do all I could to help her. I knew God's answer, but not His timing.

I called the doctor and said I thought that Char needed a special duty nurse that night, and requested one. He seemed a bit surprised and didn't think her condition merited it but kindly ordered one up.

The night was so black, I mused , as I looked out of the hospital window. I felt that something oppressive hung over the whole place. I tried to shake it off, reasoning that I was so tired, but it still hung on. I sensed that something evil was entering the hospital to get at

Char. I shuddered. Maybe I would feel better when the special duty nurse came on at 11:00pm.

When I saw the nurse, stark fear went through me. She looked like a witch. I felt like evil was somehow coming through her. She was a young woman, nice looking, with dark black hair. Nothing in her outward appearance looked evil. Rather, I sensed an evil aura about her. I shuddered. She was to be Char's special nurse.

(I might add here that I am not given to observations about people, or their "auras" or other such manifestations.)

I went to the floor lounge and pondered what to do. I had hired this nurse so that I could go to my sister's house and sleep. I had to pay her. Yet I couldn't leave her with Char. Char seemed so very vulnerable.

I went out to the desk and honestly told the nurses on duty that I didn't feel comfortable with this nurse. They tried to reassure me that she was a good nurse and maybe appeared a little haggard because she had just come off duty.

I decided to stay the night in Char's room, feeling that that was all I could do. My mind was racing, my heart was pounding, and I was continually praying, such was the fear I felt in the presence of evil. I got a blanket and covered up on the lounge chair, putting it in a reclining position. I feigned sleep, but kept one eye open.

Char was breathing heavily, almost labored. Only a dim light was on in the room.

When the nurse got up and went out on break I got up and peeked in her open carrying bag. In it was a grapefruit and a book; a new version of the *Bible*. I was confused. Could I be terribly mistaken? Yet the feeling of oppression hung on.

I tried to doze a bit, but every time the nurse moved I was wide awake. In the middle of the night she went to give Char a shot. Just before she gave the shot she turned and looked a long look in my direction. I was scared. A chill went through me. She gave the shot, and Char seemed OK.

I was relieved when morning finally came and she went off duty. I had never felt, before or since, such a strong presence of evil.

Later that day, when the doctors came in they felt that Char's condition was worsening and that she should be admitted to the ICU. At that time the family was called in.

Some time later, after the whole ordeal was over and Char had come through it, I mentioned my feelings and observations about this special duty nurse to her. This same nurse had been in the ICU with Char. She told me that, even in her semi-conscious state in the ICU, she remembered this very nurse and had bad vibes about her whenever she was around. She felt the same way I did. Evil was present.

Charmaine was stabilized in the ICU and the next day returned to her room. She became conscious, or semi-conscious, but had a totally evil look in her eyes, which I could not bear to see. She spoke in a voice not her own, rapidly counting backward, cursing Bob Sullivan (a bitter young man she knew who had hemophilia), making hissing noises, and making bleating noises exactly like a goat. She held out her arm and made circles with one finger. She appeared to me to be demon-possessed; spewing out venom. It was like it wasn't really her but some creature that had taken her over and dwelt inside.

Her arms were stiffening out and raising up. Our son-in-law Gary (Kris' husband), who had had some experience with drug-related incidents was working with her to relax her arms. She kept insisting that she had to have a specific cross or key. But it was a "no win" situation in figuring it out. Her condition worsened. Gary sat by her, talking strongly to keep her focused. I continually prayed that the Lord would give Gary the strength to continue.

The nurses on night duty didn't seem to know what to do. They quickly came and went with frightened looks on their faces.

Hours dragged on and it seemed like we weren't making any headway. But then suddenly Char's own voice broke through telling Gary, very clearly, to keep on – that he was helping her. Then she went back into the depths again, speaking in a frightening male voice. Gary and I agreed that we were witnessing a spiritual battle.

We got the Bible and looked up about spiritual warfare in Ephesians 6 and read it aloud. We weren't sure how to apply it, but knew that we could use the shield of faith spoken of in that passage, as a protection against evil.

I was terrified and couldn't bear to look at Char. It wasn't her. The Lord very clearly gave me a task to do, and that was, I felt, to open the gates of heaven. I focused on praying over and over the prayer from Revelation 7:12. "Praise and glory and wisdom and thanksgiving and honor and power and strength be to our God for ever and ever," and, "You are worthy, our Lord and God, to receive glory and honor and power, for you created all things, and by your will they are created and have their being." (Rev. 4:11)

These were scriptures that I had learned before. Now the Lord led me to repeat them over and over. I must have repeated them hundreds and hundreds of times. I imagined myself hand in hand with Jesus flying way up into heaven to open the gates. Because I had this vision, I thought that Char was dying and that I was opening the gates with Jesus for her to go through. This was my focus.

I continued praying for the Lord to give Gary strength as he was working so hard to keep her from slipping into the abyss, and to get her free from whatever was pulling her down.

I remember thinking that if we could only last until daylight things would be OK.

Then daylight came and things didn't get better – only worse.

Char got violent – punching the nurses- kicking one leg straight up and then the other. She became very strong, supernaturally so. She seemed determined to pull out her Hickman line that went directly to her heart. Gary stopped her by holding her down. She starting screaming over and over, "Mom, Mom, M-o-m." The nurses tied her hands down. She then let out a blood-curdling scream that sounded like it came out of the depths of hell – a soul in utter torment.

I couldn't stand it and ran out into the hall yelling, 'Take her Jesus, oh please take her!"

Then Char went into a catatonic state, motionless, staring without blinking.

I called the doctor from the front desk phone, getting a young intern, and told him that he had to do something. He ordered up a muscle relaxant.

About that time I gave up and begged God to take her. Gary had gone down to the chapel. Everything seemed in chaos.

Then my mother came into the hospital and calmly sat down beside Char's bed, not looking at her. She told me later that she simply stated the truth of Char's being; that she was perfect as God had created her.

A doctor came in. He asked Charmaine her name and she said,

"I'm Charmaine Mosher, a student at the vet school." Her mind was clear! Miraculously, wondrously, unbelievably, she was out of the clutches of evil.

She had a few slight relapses the next few days but for the most part was her normal self.

The next day Char had a young minister come in from The Way ministry to give us Communion. We both wept tears of relief. God had rescued her. We had grateful hearts.

Char thought that perhaps God had healed her. We took her home on Saturday. The next day was Easter Sunday: Resurrection Day. Char did very well for the next two weeks. We hoped that she was healing and would regain her full strength.

I believed that somehow a great spiritual battle was taking place that Easter week. Things were going on in the heavenly realms of which we were only a small part. I can't help but think that it was no coincidence that it happened on Holy Week or that God used us in this battle.

After we arrived home, I experienced a state of mental, physical, and spiritual exhaustion. I felt unable to function. My skin even felt heavy – like it was hanging on me and weighing me down. I couldn't pray. An inner voice took over, softly telling me what to do. "Get out of bed. Go to the closet. See that blouse. Put it on." I obeyed, moving slowly like a robot, without feeling, throughout the day. The rest of the family bustled around, unaware, and went on their way. I was able to slowly pack the children's lunches and send them to school. I drew back from any contact with anyone. If one more thing happened, I felt, it would push me over the cliff. I knew it. I laid down to rest often, doing only that work which was absolutely necessary. The next day a booklet arrived in the mail from a colleague whom I knew only from conference meetings. That booklet was exactly what I needed. One side of the page had simple words about how one might feel during illness. The other side of the page had corresponding scriptures written out. The words strengthened me and I began to return to my normal self.

Spiritual warfare is exhausting. It requires rest afterwards and time of refreshing. In the Bible we read that the angels came and took care of Jesus after his exhausting conflict with Satan in the desert (Matt. 4). I was thankful that God gave me that rest. Many good people had been praying for me at that time, or I might have fallen into illness.

Conversely, Char had come home from that experience exhilarated. She said that she had had to go to hell to fight Satan and the Lord had made her strong enough. Although I had thought that she was separated from her Maker during that time, she said, "No. God was always there."

Now, she felt much better and hoped that she might be healed. She had her horse brought down from Cornell and kept in a barn down the road. She was hopeful that she would recover over the summer and go back to Cornell in the fall.

She tried. She was better than she had been in a long time. She began helping a neighbor with a 4-H group involved with horses. She gained some weight.

But then the old problems came back, like strong, unruly forces that had been contained for a while but now regrouped to attack again. By the end of the summer she was almost blind – a bitter pill to swallow. If it was only the blindness, she would have gotten herself a seeing-eye dog and gone on in college and maybe become a professor. But she was weak and ill. She had to drive herself to even get out of bed in the morning and get going. Usually by afternoon she was better.

She was having laser treatments on her eyes every few weeks. She couldn't draw anymore, nor could she play the guitar, as she had depended on reading the notes. She couldn't see her horse very well either. What a cruel blow. One treasure given to her only to be taken away so soon. "The Lord giveth and the Lord taketh away" (Job 1:21). Only God knows his reasons. We mourned her loses.

Chapter 16

Ivar

"I will send my angels and they will watch over you"
(Psalm 91:11)

Again God sent Char an animal. Ivar. He was a large, male Doberman dog. I smilingly thought of him as a big black devil lurking around my kitchen. He looked like one to me; flat head, eyes too far back on the side of his face, a mouth that stretched from ear to ear and teeth that said that one swipe could finish off your jugular vein. I didn't want to get too close to him.

Somehow we always got sucked into keeping the animals that Char attracted, and brought home, so I guess I shouldn't have been surprised at a Doberman.

Our nephew, who could no longer keep him, dropped the dog off at our house because Char reasoned that "everyone wanted a Doberman," and the vet next door could surely find a home for him.

But weeks went by. All those people that wanted Dobermans seemed to have gone into hiding. By now Ivar had chosen his owner. Charmaine. Char, who had hoped to be going back to vet school at Cornell in the fall. Char, who had hoped her eyes would be getting better rather than worse. Char, whose body, we had hoped, would be getting stronger, but seemed to be getting weaker.

Now began a series of eye operations for Char. The massive chemotherapy that she had taken for a fungus infection (histoplasmosis) had thrown her diabetes out of control. The doctors thought that this might be the reason for loss of eyesight.

One morning, when I came into her room, she was lying in bed

93

looking out the window. Her voice was questioning, "Mom, when I look out the window everything looks red. It's not red outdoors, is it?" I wanted to weep. She was bleeding into her eyes, and despite all efforts to stop it, it continued.

Trusty Ivar continued to be a source of amazement. Char had taken him to a few obedience training classes when she had felt better. She said, "Mom. We have to make eye contact with our dogs from a distance. I can't even see Ivar, but he sits right there and obeys the commands. It's like he was trained before."

As her eyes got worse, Char began to count the steps to the barn – so many down the sidewalk, then turn onto the dirt driveway – so many more down to the barn. A neighbor had made her a cane with a metal tip to tap on the sidewalk. She was determined to work with her horse, but the constant diarrhea interfered, as well as her eyesight loss. One day she came home crying, "I couldn't even put the saddle on Dancer. I couldn't tell her front from her rear."

Ivar began to lead her. One morning, looking out the bedroom window, I saw him out in front of her, on his leash, leading her around a huge mud puddle. "How did he know how to do that," I wondered?

Char lay on the couch much of the day, and Ivar laid on the floor beside her, head down on his two front paws, looking morose.

Fall came and the bottom fell out of Char's world. She had told all her friends that she would be returning to classes in the fall. Now she called it a postponement. "I'm going to have more laser treatments on my eyes," she told them, "and when they get better, I'll be back." The university kept her place at vet school open for her.

Ivar became more protective than ever of Char. His eye was always upon her and he wouldn't leave her side. Char quipped, "He's the only male that was ever madly in love with me."

One day Ivar growled and leaped up at one of our son Russell's friends. "For no reason at all, Mom, he almost attacked Brian." Another incident happened. Our year old grandson toddled on shaky legs across the living room toward where Charmaine was sitting. Suddenly Ivar was there, his head thrust forward, lips drawn all the way back to show his canine incisors, a low growl in his throat. He threatened. We shouted and grabbed Ivar and spanked him and banned him to the playroom. I didn't like it.

"Mom, I'll make sure that Ivar doesn't hurt anybody. I'll keep my hand right on his collar when anybody comes." Char assured me.

"Lord," I prayed, "don't let this dog bring us to any grief."

Char's trips to the barn became fewer. She spent most of her days on the couch with Ivar by her side. Then it was time for another eye operation. Char and I packed up her things to take her the hundred miles to the hospital where surgery was to be done, starting with her right eye. A last ditch stand to save her vision. She said good-by to Ivar. He laid there, his dark head on the floor. He never moved. Only his eyes followed her out the door.

Several days went by. The operation was over. I arrived home late one evening. Char was still in the hospital resting comfortably, with hopes that her sight would return when the swelling went down.

I opened the front door, sad and tired. Ivar leaped up to meet me and raced around and around me. He poked his nose out the door and dashed out to circle the car. No Charmaine. He tore off into the night despite my calls after him. "Come back, Ivar!" I started to unpack.

The door-bell rang and a distraught man met me at the front door. "Just hit a dog with my van. I'm so sorry! Neighbor says it's your dog."

"Oh Ivar! Ivar!" We ran down the street to where he lay by the side of the road. He looked at us with glassy eyes. Ron knelt down to comfort him. I raced to get the vet.

Doc shook his head. "Nope, nothing I can do. His back is broken. Better put him out of his misery. It's the best thing you can do."

"Oh Ivar! Why'd you have to leap in front of a car? Why'd you have to get yourself killed?"

Char took the news better than we expected. "He was such a nice dog. I always did want a Doberman."

Andrea:
Most clearly, I remember when dad and I went to see Char in the hospital after Ivar died. She said she was awakened in the night by the sound of tires screeching and a "thump." When we told her Ivar was killed, she already knew.

****

The thought again came to me, "The Lord giveth and the Lord

taketh away." I really didn't understand why Char had to lose this beloved pet. So many gifts in her life had been given, only to be suddenly snatched away. Then I remembered my prayer that Ivar bring us to no grief. Perhaps his death was the Lord's way of sparing us another grief.

I had always called Ivar a black devil, but for this time in Char's life he had certainly been an angel in disguise.

As time went on, God was again speaking to my heart and changing my prayers. His words were, "I am bringing into completion that which I began in her" (Philippians 1:6). I felt in my heart that she would die. Now it seemed that I should pray that she might have the strength to endure. This seemed to be very important. I believe that this "endurance" was spiritual endurance. Lastly, the prayer given to me was that God's glory might be seen in her.

Chapter 17

Good-bye Yellow Brick Road

"a time to plant and a time to uproot"
(Ecclesiastes 3:2b)

Again, I had to learn to live one day at a time. I began to be tormented by thoughts of Char's death. I would see her sitting in the rocking chair and would think, "One day that chair will be empty. She'll be gone." I had thoughts of her funeral. Bad feelings followed me around. And here she was, alive! This was not the time to grieve. I had to work at chasing all the negative thoughts out of my mind.

Gloria came home from college and got us all in a good mood. Char had wanted another monkey so Gloria joked about Char becoming a beggar, sitting on the street corner with a monkey who held the tin cup. Laughter was so good. It kept us afloat.

The family cat would unexpectedly jump upon Char's lap for a petting. A gentle comfort. Another of God's "angels."

Char and I had many talks about God. She accepted everything in her life as coming from His hand. She knew that He had a purpose even if we couldn't always see it. She had a strong belief that God had told her that she would see "better than before" and that she would become a vet. She hung onto these promises with an iron grip.

The laser treatments had not worked, nor had an eye operation. Ron and I were skeptical about her having any more eye operations because each time, following surgery, she went into pneumonia and other complications, besides having to have many transfusions at home. We wondered, too, if the young doctor wasn't experimenting.

But Char insisted that they should keep trying. She had been made a part of the medical team.

Sitting by her hospital bedside during her recovery after surgery, the same Alton John song, popular at the time, played repeatedly on the radio; "Good-bye yellow brick road, where the dogs of society howl. You can't plant me in your penthouse, I'm going back to my plow. Back to the howlin' old owl in the woods, huntin' the horney-back toad … my future lies beyond the yellow brick road, oo, oo, oo." Somehow, it always seemed that song was for her. Her future wasn't here.

Prayers kept going out for Char. Her best friend in college put a little stone in her shoe so that as she walked about the campus it would irritate her foot and remind her to pray for Char.

Christmas came and Char sent me traipsing through stores to get gifts for friends and a favorite professor. Nothing would do but a blown-glass winged horse for him. I placed it in her hands so she could feel it. She was excited and insisted I get it sent right out. Her elation over these endeavors out-weighed my weariness.

Up until Christmas, Char could see just a little light, enough to tell where windows were. But shortly after Christmas, she entered a world of gray darkness.

Chapter 18

The Long Night Is Almost Over

"---weeping may remain for a night, but rejoicing comes in the morning."
(Psalm 30:5)

Still there were more eye operations. What little sight there had been in her "good" eye was now taken away, since it was that eye's turn to be operated on.

Charmaine began to be perturbed over her deteriorating condition. Her attitude was that the doctors were missing something. What was wrong? We weren't getting answers.

The news of the HIV virus had hit the newspapers. The country was in near hysteria over this mysterious virus. Tests were being taken. Research was being done.

I went to see Char's favorite nurse. We talked for a while and I asked her what was wrong with Char. What the doctors, who cared so much about Charmaine, had been unable to tell us, she now told me. "Char has now been diagnosed as having AIDS." That had been in the back of our minds for weeks. Now it was out. AIDS, the killer. No treatment. No survivors. The worst was now a reality.

The next big question was, should we tell Char? Some family members said, "No, she'll give up all hope if you tell her." I prayed very hard for several days over this question that agonized me. The answer that came back was that it was really not a matter of great importance whether we told her or not.

Char was recovering from the eye surgery and asking me a lot of questions. I kept hedging, and didn't like being in the position of

99

having to tell her little lies concerning her condition. Finally I told her, "The doctors have now diagnosed you with AIDS." It was a shock, but I think she expected it. Her strong answer was, "Well, I don't agree with their diagnosis." I made no reply.

When Char came home again, for her weakness, the doctors ordered up transfusions of whole blood, to be given at our small local hospital.

On a January night, Char was having trouble walking as I helped her to the emergency room door. The wind and snow swirled around us, beating against us as I struggled with opening the door. A voice said, almost audibly, to me, "The long night is almost over." I knew her suffering was not going to drag on for a long time.

In February, Char had to go to the city hospital again. She was feeling badly but still insisting that she was going to get better. We could not broach the subject of her possible death. Therefore we could neither comfort her nor weep with her. Difficult as that was, I realized it was her way of being strong.

One day I took Russell out of school and brought him up to see her. At age sixteen he had spent a lot of his free time with Char, talking with her in her room at home. His presence at the hospital on a school day, missing basketball practice, signified to Char our grave concern over her. When he left the room, she was angry with me. "You don't have to keep coming up here everyday. I'm going to be OK." My response to her was, in effect, that she'd better start thinking about how she was treating people, in case she didn't make it. I left, feeling badly on all counts.

Since we had no idea how much time Char had, perhaps several months, Ron and I took turns going up to the hospital to stay with her. The school continued to let him use his accumulated sick days as days off, and I juggled my church schedule to fit the time. Her sisters and brothers and aunts and uncles and grandmother all came to sit with her and take turns being with her.

Ron had a fear that he would not be with her when she died. I prayed that he would be there. Somehow I felt at peace that it would work out just as God wanted it to.

On Sunday evening that week Ron had been with her and arrived home around 10pm., very worried that maybe he shouldn't have come home.

At midnight a nurse called and said that Char had taken a turn for the worse. Char had told her that she was dying and to call her parents. We jumped in the car and sped the hundred miles back up to the hospital, thankful that the winter roads were OK.

When we got there Char was in a lot of pain. She told us that she was dying. She told us that she loved us. She named off each of her brothers and sisters and said to tell them that she loved them. She said with enthusiasm "I had a great life." She expressed how wonderful God was/is. She gave instructions that she wanted no resuscitation, no going into the ICU, no attempts to keep her alive.

She told her father, "Turn toward God now, Dad, not away from God." She was concerned over the effect her death would have on him.

True to form, she made provision for her animals: her horse's foal, when it was born, was to go to the neighbor lady where she kept her horse. A stuffed toy bulldog was to go to a favorite nurse, who had shared a joke with her over it concerning a flirtatious male intern. For a few other things, she had small requests.

When she got all done, she thought she would die, but she didn't. Because she was in awful pain she began to lament, "This could take days and I can't stand it." I assured her that it wouldn't. I felt so totally helpless that I couldn't help her in her pain. The thought came to me to rub her back. I had her lie on her side while I rubbed her back. It seemed to distract the pain a bit.

We stayed with her, constantly telling her how much we loved her, that she was a beautiful person in our lives, that we were happy she had been born to us, that she was a blessing to us.

The doctors were still taking tests, trying to find something that would make her more comfortable.

The day wore on. My mother and sister came over. Our daughter, Kris, and her husband, Gary, came up again. Gary was one of Char's favorite people. He had been very supportive of her in the last months, sitting next to her at Christmas, his arm around her shoulders, kidding her, making her laugh, enjoying her company.

By Monday night Ron and I were exhausted. We had been awake since Sunday morning. A cot was brought into her hospital room for us and we took turns resting on it.

Char needed constant care, which the family was primarily

providing. She was restless and so we worked to get her comfortable. She was weak and vomiting every little while. Ron and I went to the hospital chapel and knelt to pray. We prayed that God would be merciful and take her soon. At one point Char brightened and said, "One good thing about this, it really brings you closer to God." Gary immediately quipped, "If you get any closer you're going to be in the pocket of his robe!" That struck us all as extremely funny. I laughed until my sides ached. Char laughed and laughed too.

Finally around midnight Kris and Gary said their good-byes to her and left.

Char had been breathing very hard, her body, restless and agitated, labored to keep her going.

Young nurses and interns came quietly into her room from time to time, faces half covered in blue surgical masks, fearful eyes darting here and there. I sat peacefully by Char's side holding her hand. God had given me great peace. I spoke softly to them, "You really don't have to wear those masks. This disease is not air borne." I felt sorry for them, having to face the death of one who was so close to their age.

The lights were dimmed. Pain medicine was given to Char and we all tried to rest.

Somewhere in the wee hours of the morning things began to change for Char. She became much more peaceful. Her body still labored to keep her going, but her manner was no longer restless.

She became very pleasant, almost happy, and she started singing. She was not a person who sang very often, so this was unusual. The hymn, "I Come To The Garden Alone" sounded melodiously from her lips. She encouraged me to sing with her so I did. Her voice was strong and clear. We sang "Amazing Grace" next, and then "Kum By A," repeating the songs several times. Char said, "I wish that I could do something for God." My answer was, "Maybe you're doing something right now."

Just then, a young nurse who had been attending Char came in and said, "I heard you singing out in the hall. You are such an inspiration to me."

In a little while I laid back down on the cot beside Ron. I could hear Char talking and mumbling in a pleasant voice. She was saying, "Oh, its beautiful. It's so beautiful."

Then, as I laid there, I became aware that I no longer heard Char breathing. I jumped up and leaned over her. Ron called for the nurse.

She was lying there, her head turned to the side, looking very much as if she were sleeping. She was gone. Gone from this life. Gone to a better place. Gone to be with her Lord. I called out to her, "Charmaine! You are free! You are free!" I held her in my arms and kissed her. Ron said his soft good-byes to her.

Dawn was breaking on that cold February morning. I looked out her window and saw hospital personnel coming into work. For them, a day like any other. For me, a huge chunk of my world was gone. But I was at peace. God had ordained it. Char had completed her work on this earth. Routine hospital work took over. Questions were asked. Papers were signed. We had to take her pitifully few things home. As I was packing them up, the Lord said to my heart, "A man's wealth does not consist in the abundance of his possessions" (Luke 12:15). How true.

Ron and I wept our tears over her, held hands and walked out to the car. Our hearts were heavy, knowing that we had to face all of our children and tell them the sad news.

Funeral arrangements were being made. The funeral director called us. Sounding upset, he requested that we come over right away.

In his office his fearful voice questioned us: Did we know that our daughter had AIDS? Yes. Well, this would require special treatment and protective clothing for the assistants. It would cost more. We said OK. He was unsure about having an open casket, and people touching the body. We reassured him that there was no danger for visitors, but suggested that he call our doctor.

In the end, he agreed to an open casket. The fear of AIDS was encompassing the country. He didn't want his usual hairdresser doing Char's hair. Kris rose to the occasion and said, "I've done her hair for her many times. I'll do it." And she did.

Kris:
While I was doing her hair I accidentally touched her head with the curling iron, and said, "Whoops, sorry!" and then laughed.

I lamented that I couldn't get her hair to look exactly as I wanted. I heard a clear thought from her, "I've always liked the way you've

done my hair. Don't worry, it'll be fine."
****

The night after Char died, exhausted as I was, I couldn't sleep. I was concerned about how Char would look "laid out." Her disease had caused her body to swell up. I knew she wouldn't want to be seen looking like that. Somewhere in the middle of the night her voice came gently to me, "Don't worry Mom, I'll look presentable."

The dress she wore was chosen by two good friends of mine. In answer to their offer to help I had sent them out to pick a dress. Pink. Long-sleeved. Not fancy. They had gone about their task prayerfully and with unusual joy, had found exactly the dress.

Because I had felt her presence speaking to me so clearly in the night, I thought that perhaps I would rely on her to guide me in some other things. When I followed this direction her clear thought came to me, "You don't need me, Mom. You've got Jesus."

"Yes, of course," I smiled. And I did not seek that contact again.

When I approached her casket for the first time to look at her, the Lord brought these words to my mind, "Why do you seek the living among the dead? She is not here. She is risen!" The words that had been spoken about Jesus.

Char's four brothers and three sisters and their spouses stood in attendance at the funeral home. Her funeral was at the Ellisburg Union Church where I served as pastor. Those gentle people had given us much comfort and support. Music played, and a wonderful dinner was set up to feed all who came.

The committal service at the cemetery was presided over by the District Superintendent; a kindly gentleman. As we stood on that cold ground, with large, fluffy snowflakes softly falling, I was again reminded that this was the kind of a day that Char liked best. A day to get the horses out and take them for a run.

Chapter 19

The Lord's Blessing

"...there will be showers of blessings"
(Ezekiel 34:26).

Cards and letters came to us from many places. Dozens of people wrote about what an inspiration Char's courage had been to them, and how their lives had drawn closer to God for knowing her. Even five years later we were receiving letters from those whose lives she had touched. They would never forget her.

I asked the family what they thought we should write on Char's gravestone. It seemed fitting she should have an epitaph. The family chose me to write it. Her stone reads:

Charmaine C. Mosher
Dec. 26, 1960-Feb. 11, 1986

SHE TAUGHT US COURAGE
DEVOTION TO GOD AND
LOVE OF HIS CREATURES
GREAT AND SMALL

Mark:
Although she was determined to the point of being bull-headed, there was a quality about Charmaine that made her stand out from those around her.

She could transport you into another world – her world where dreams and opportunities were just around the corner. She so easily

105

drew you into the excitement of her life. Talking with her made you feel a part of them. I don't recall that she ever needed attention or demanded the spotlight. Everyone was welcome to participate in her visions and share in their rewards. I think that Charmaine naturally connected people to something greater than the island each of us calls "self."

****

Andrea:

I remember that Char was always very loving and interested in what I was doing. She was a great example to me. Her physical problems didn't slow her down, why should mine slow me down?

When I turned 25 I thought, "Well, this is how old Char was when she died." I felt bad that she never got to be married or have a career. But when I think about it, I don't believe she was meant for that. She touched those around her in a very special way and inspired us with her faith in God. She showed us how beautiful life is and how to treasure each moment and those around us.

****

Winter did not seem to last long, and in the spring Ron and I heard that a foal had been born to a horse, Dancer, that Char had taken to Ithaca to breed.

Our hearts were drawn to travel to Ithaca, to the barns where Char had worked, and see this little foal for which she had had so much anticipation.

The day we arrived was pleasant, but with enough of a nip in the air to merit wearing a sweatshirt. We hung over the rail fence, looking out across acres of pasture, empty but interspersed with trees and scrub brush. No Dancer, no foal, as far as the eye could see.

Luba, the barn tender commented, "Oh, Dancer must have gone on down to the far pasture. I don't know if you'll get to see her. Sometimes they stay down there for days."

Disappointment and sadness filled us as we stood around the barn. What to do? We had been there a half-hour or more, and who knew when or if the horse and foal would come back.

I wistfully breathed a little prayer. We did so want to be a part of this new life.

Suddenly, at the far end of the field, we saw her coming. Galloping, galloping, mane and tail flying out behind her, Dancer came racing across the meadows towards us. And behind her running her new-born legs off, a little black foal.

My heart leaped for joy. They came right up to our fence and stood for us to "oh and ah" over them. Luba provided us with grain for Dancer. With arms outstretched, we stroked Dancer and spoke in soft voices to her, "Here girl, what a beautiful foal you have."

It was a happy time. The Lord's grace for our wounded souls. A little bit of Char returned, for one bright afternoon. Ron and I went home refreshed.

Another incident occurred six years later as I was driving alone in the car on my way to be with my sister a few days before her surgery. As I was driving along, listening to my Christian music tapes, Char came strongly into my imagination. I saw her clearly.

Mentally, I inquired what she was doing. She answered that she was working on dressage. Dressage? Oh yes, the training of horses to prance (step) kind of sideways to music, I remembered.

I wondered about Robin. Char said, "Oh, Robby is here with me." A little girl of about six or seven came and stood close beside Char. Char put her arm around her neck.

They seemed to have an understanding that I did not. The ability for me to understand their existence was hidden from me, but my life was clear to them. They had a realization of my earthly life. They were so happy.

It seemed to me that I saw a long road ahead – my life – and that Char indicated that there would be many people that I would help.

I wish that I had better words in explaining this vision. Char and Robin seemed to be on a higher plane of existence. It was as if from their perspective they could evaluate my life here, perhaps as a lower stage of being, but a necessary one. They saw me without personal emotion, a good kind of detachment.

Then they were on the horse, bareback, Char in front, Robin in back.

Following, I saw a front view of them on the horse. The horse was side-stepping to the music. Char had a big grin on her face. Her wonderful grin of *joie de vie*!

Then they were gone.

A great surge of heartache, mixed with desire for them went over me.

My spirit agonized and I cried and cried. I missed them so.

Yet when that passed, I felt a pleasant sense of peace. I felt blessed by this treasure given to me. It has been in my mind since – a wonderful glimpse into life here-after. Sometime I will see them again.

The day was April 9, the anniversary of Robin's birth.

Amen

God has been so good to me. Although I have written much more about our sorrows than our joys perhaps it is because we learn more from our sorrows. They will be an important part of Charmaine's name in God's book of life, and mine in His book, as well. For now the pain of the sorrows has faded. The joy remains!